AXIS OF EVIL
PERFORATED PRAETER NATURAM

Stamp Art Navigated and Curated by **Michael Hernandez de Luna**

Book Design by **Brandtner Design**

QUALIATICA PRESS

Art Direction and Design
Al Brandtner
Michael Hernandez de Luna

Associate Designer
Maria Dimanshtein

Production
Eric Hofmeister
Veronica KeHoss
Bekah Peterson

www.brandtnerdesign.com

Printed in South Korea
by asianprinting.com

Qualiatica Press, Chicago 60647
www.qualiatica.com
© 2004 Qualiatica Press
All Rights Reserved. Published 2004
International Standard Book Number
ISBN 0-9753096-090000

Miriam: Take evil by the tail

And you find you are holding good

head-downwards

— **CHRISTOPHER FRY**

IN THE FALL OF 2003 QUALIATICA DECIDED TO STAGE AN ART SHOW AND CREATE A series of visual and written dialogues on the mythology of Evil, titled *Axis of Evil*. After discussions with stamp artist Michael Hernandez de Luna, who had curated and navigated a recent show called *Sextablos*, Qualiatica decided to commission de Luna to perform a similar function. The result is this visually exciting and thought-provoking assemblage of art from around the world, all in stamp format.

Postal stamp art provides a unique medium for exploring individual and cultural visions of evil. This group of artworks will be touring the world for several years and this book and the accompanying DVD are meant to complement the art while also providing separate formats for Perforating the Praeter Naturam of Evil.

Multimedia wiz Al Brandtner and his associates at Brandtner Design have created the book that is before you and writer-activist Warren Leming has worked with the documentary filmmakers at BulletProof Film to create the DVD.

Evil resides not in the world, but in our perceptions of the world around us. We hope that these works of art, essays and the DVD cause you to explore the folk myths we hide behind and which mediate our worldview.

JIM SWANSON • *Qualiatica*

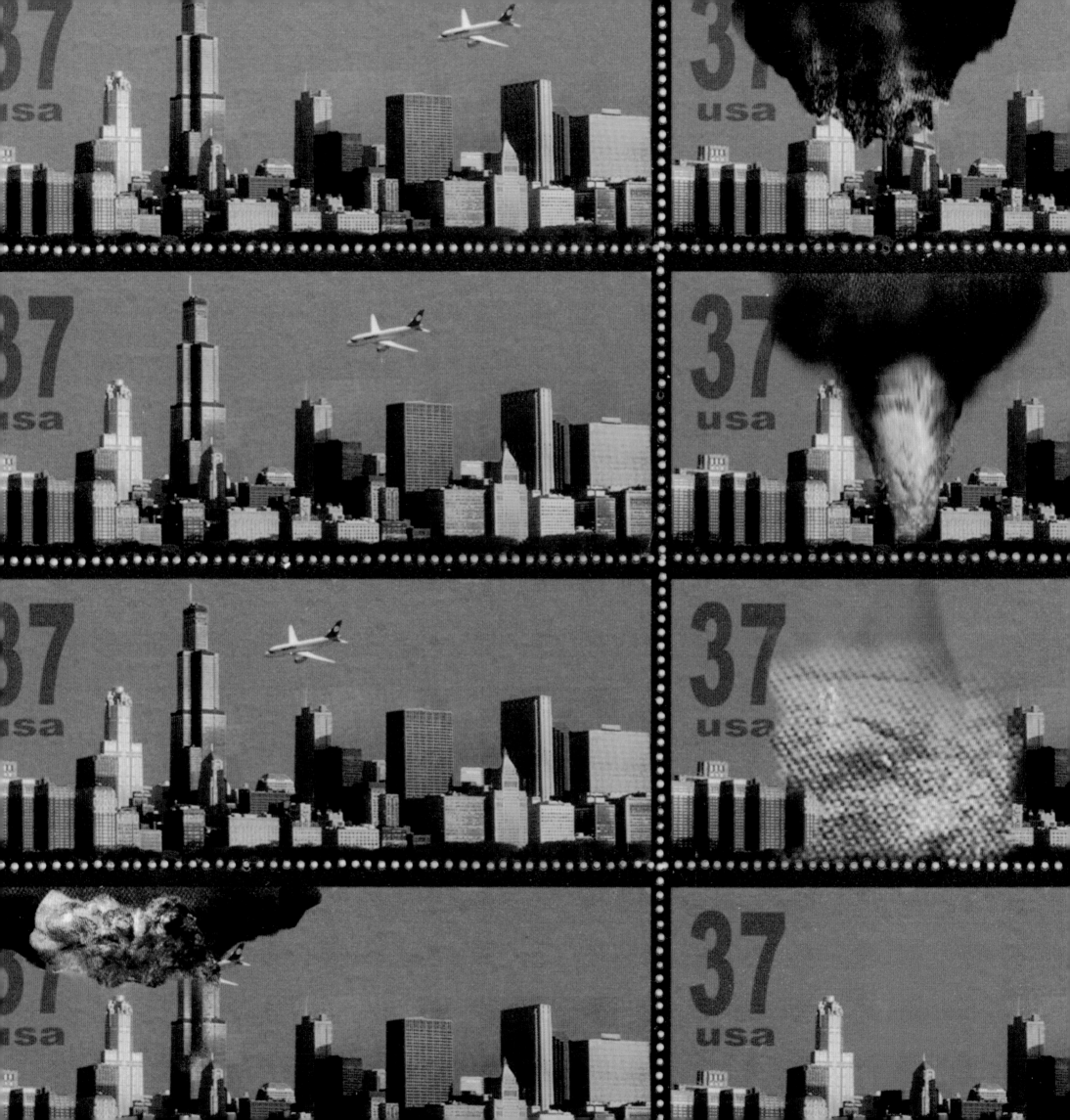

IN THE FALL OF 2003 THE DIRECTOR OF QUALIATICA,

Jim Swanson, approached me to Curate and Navigate an exhibition we named: *Axis of Evil: Perforated Praeter Naturam.* Our ideas were to shed light on the myths of evil and its doers through the philatelic art of the Postage Stamp and literature. Our many discussions peg evil: first existing only within the perimeters of religious belief, and second, mythical and non-existing in a psychological mindset.

Now, how do you shed light on this evil madness? For me, it's inviting a colorful array of 54 international artists and writers from 11 countries to help us assemble this body of work and book. We've asked our collaborators to show us what they see as Evil and interpret this through the Artist's Stamp Sheet and a handful of essays.

The results are a visual labyrinth in social commentary with seven individual outlooks and viewpoints melding in Pop Culture, Philately, and Protest.

As curator and organizer, navigator and artist, I am convinced there is no one definition to this question of evil; each one of us has our own definitions, views, and concepts. Each one of us has a face for our demons and monsters. Each one of us sees and justifies morality in our own light. And every one of us is capable of being as petty and rotten; as the bums we love to hate. So therefore, this book is incomplete by omission of your unseen images and thoughts on this topic.

The Frankensteins, Medusas, and the Boogeymen of the classic horror tale have morphed into the human face of an endless stream of everyday Villains: Housewives, CEOs, Priests, Mechanics, Politicians, Children, and City Employees just to list a few. … Our environment has become the breeding ground for psychos and fanatics bent on disrupting life. My image of the world is that it has always been barbaric, primitive, and cruel. And this amazes me for being the 21st century; we cannot find a solution for peace. — **MICHAEL HERNANDEZ DE LUNA** • Chicago • April 1, 2004

14

15

"The universe is not only queerer than we suppose, but queerer than we can suppose....I suspect that there are more things in heaven and earth than are dreamed of, in any philosophy."

– J.B.S. Haldane

17

22

16

20

18

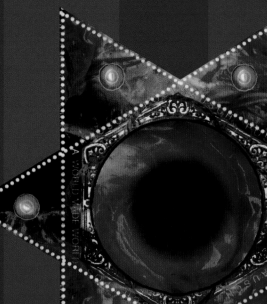

24

28

29

12

13

TERROR

19

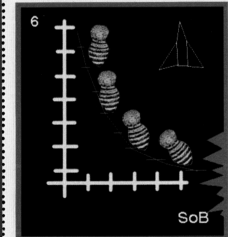

23

TRANS-IRATE
2003
WAR POLI
£¥€ Ø
DOGFISH
$

21

THIS
STAMP
KILLS
FASCISTS
USA ★37

25

If you create
art, you're an
artist. S.Sch

AMLPOST

26

27

TTT POST - Regular Issue - 2004
Published by FIVE/CINQ Unlimited
West Vancouver, British Columbia, CANADA

1/5

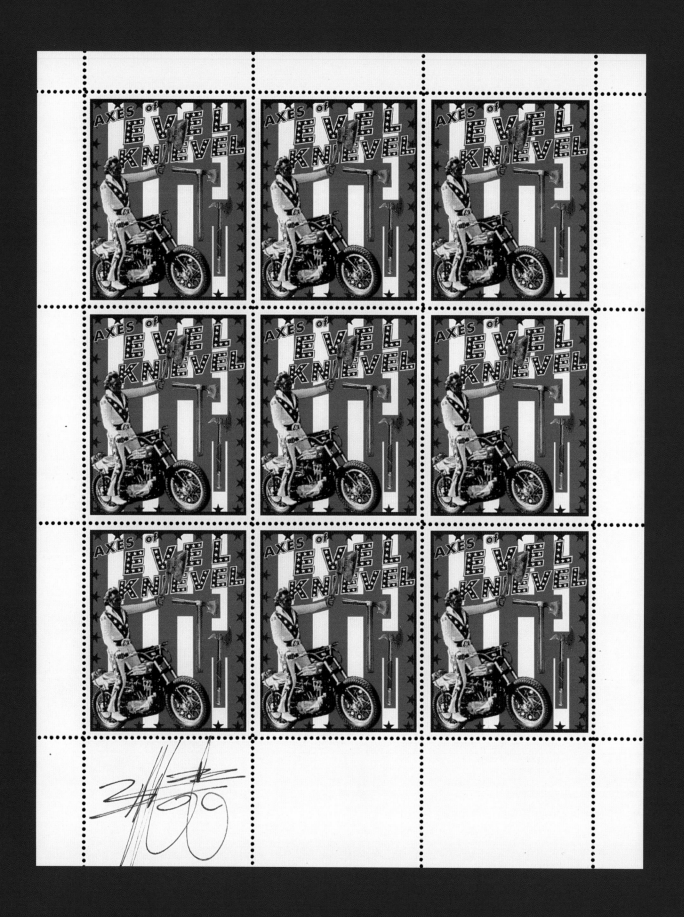

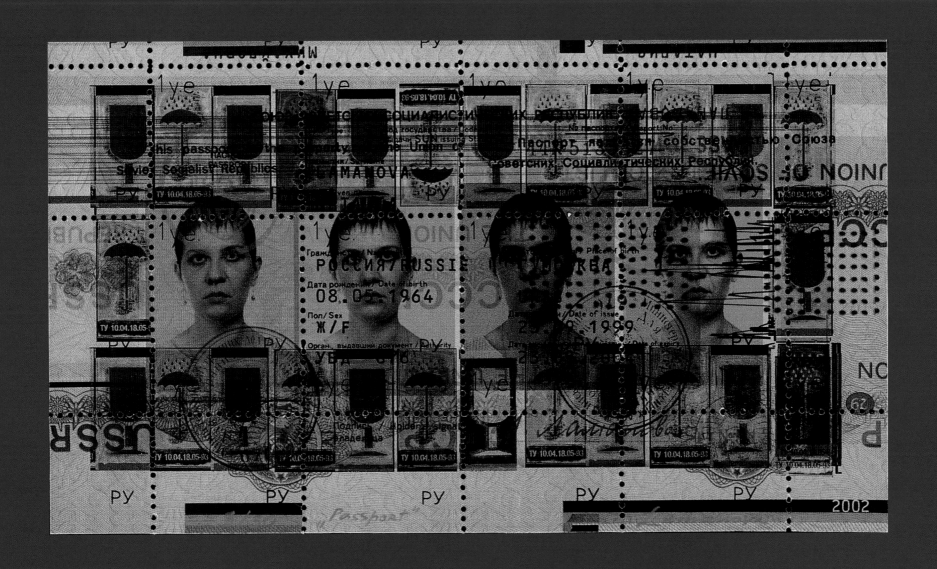

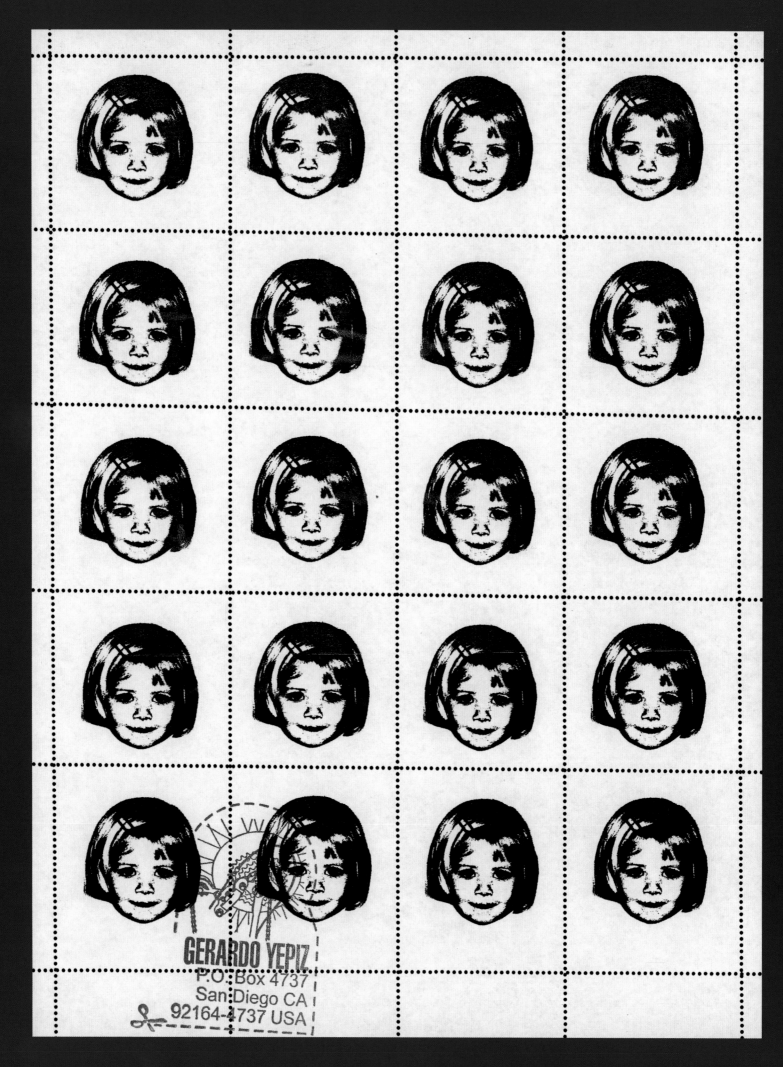

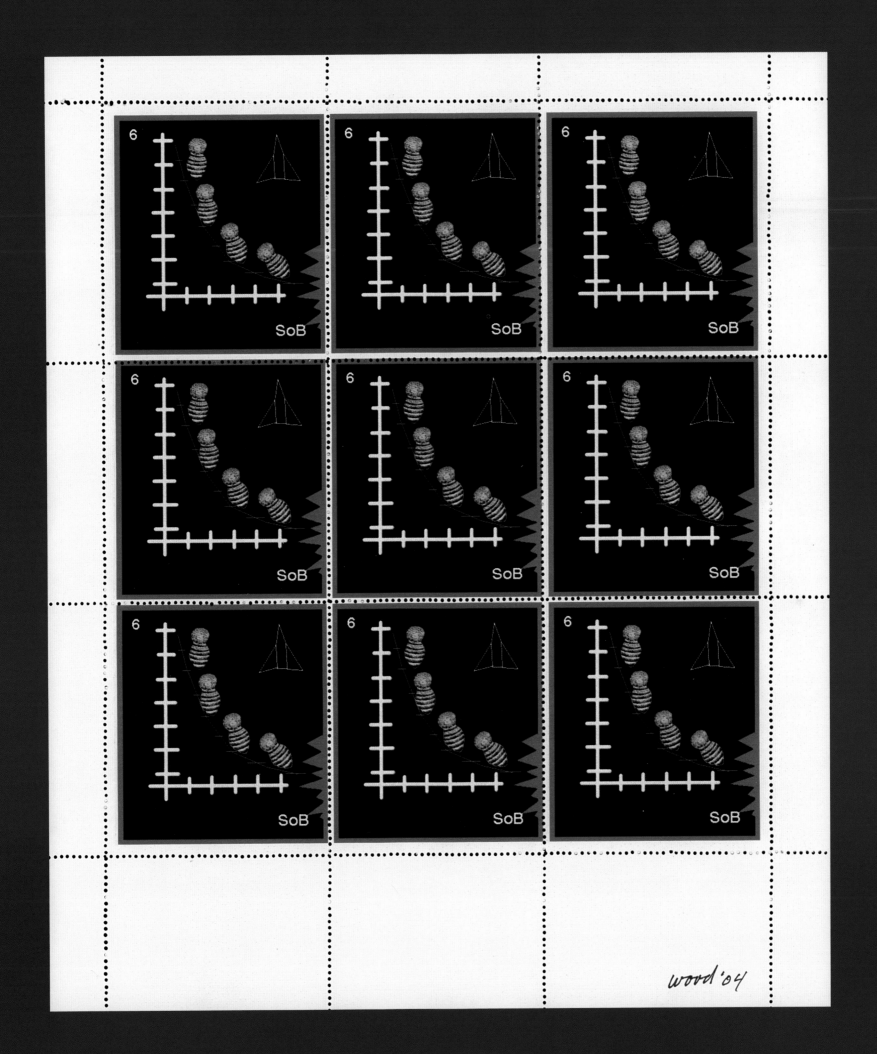

wood '04

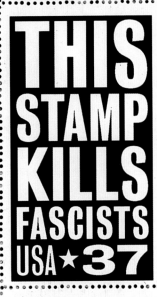

TTT POST - SPECIAL ISSUE - 2004
Published by FIVE/CINQ Unlimited

1/5

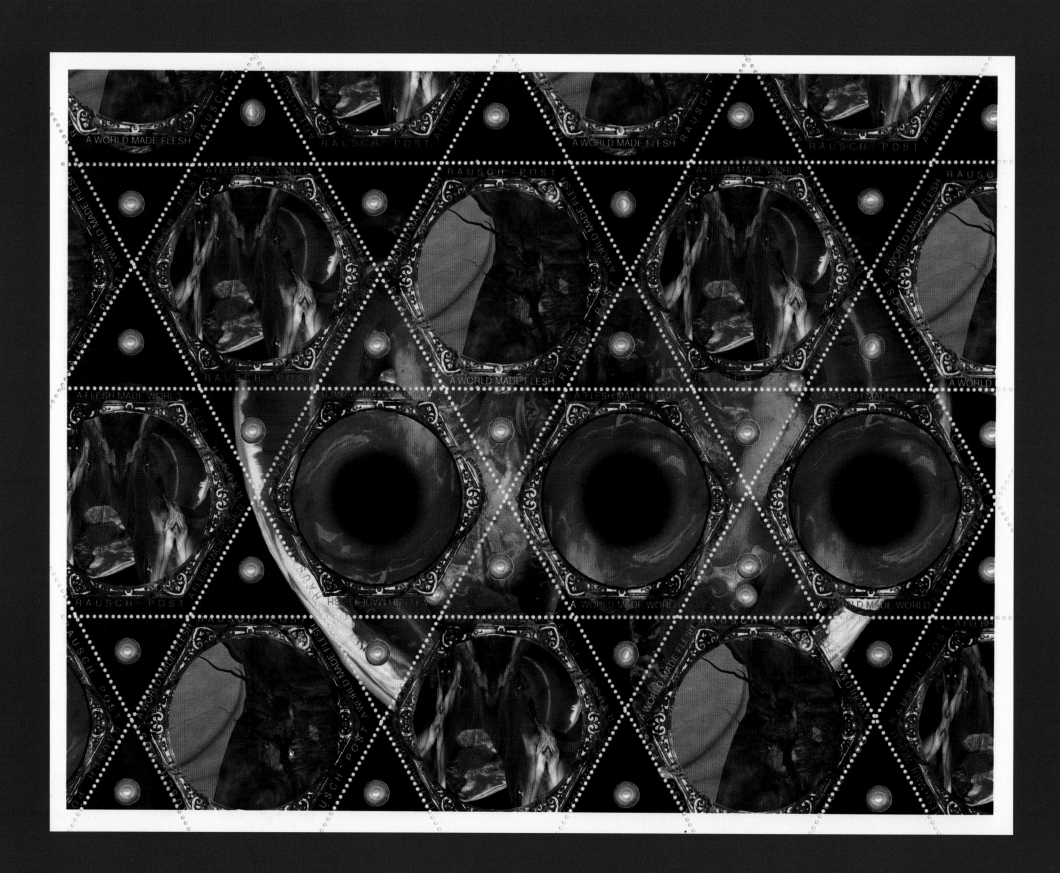

artistamp@egroups.com

DELETE 47 USA

Sorry but I just don't care for opening email where someone writes such as Fricker and Merlin have and (if I'd like to stay on the list) going to have to tolerate this. K.M.

AML POST

DELETE 47 USA

In my opinion, people who resort to this form of expression don't have the intelligence or vocabulary to express themselves other-wise, thus giving off the odiferous air of ignorance. S.V.

AML POST

DELETE 47 USA

.. rather the tone and feelings the communications generate are not at all welcome and quickly deleted from my "inbox", then deleted from deleting to insure they are deleted from my world. A nice clean way to get rid of an annoying person! C.A.D.

AML POST

DELETE 47 USA

I just blocked his address. Now I can enjoy the list without being riled up by people who like (and seem to live for) antagonizing people. A.

AML POST

DELETE 47 USA

And another option, Karen, is just to delete Merlin and Fricker when they show up on your email list as I do. Kat

AML POST

DELETE 47 USA

I too have had enough of this tiny brain and testicle diatribe coming from members of this group. The old saying that one bad apple spoils the barrel is true. G.B.

AML POST

DELETE 47 USA

If I see anything more of the sort from you, I guarantee, it will be the last message of yours I read. R.S.

AML POST

DELETE 47 USA

I realize that the European art world is even more regimented than the US one, but the idea that you can't call yourself an artist until you have been validated by an outside authority seems pretty silly to me. S.Sch.

AML POST

If you create art, you're an artist. S.Sch

AML POST

DELETE 47 USA

DELETE 47 USA

DELETE 47 USA

Remember, you have the right and the capability to filter out or delete email before it is read, if you so desire. It is a very effective means of not exposing yourself to something that you might consider offensive or harmful to yourself. The other alternative is to state your opinion every time you encounter something you do not like. You are free to do that. Greg **AML POST**

H.R.Fricker 5. JUNI 2000 ONE YEAR OF ARTISTAMP MAILING LIST ON INTERNET ISSUE

© United Suspected Artists

08.02.04

67/200

26 • Moscow (Capitol of the World) • **SLAVA VINOGRADOV** • MOSCOW-RUSSIA

David Gilhooly

JUST SO MUCH TOILET PAPER

2003

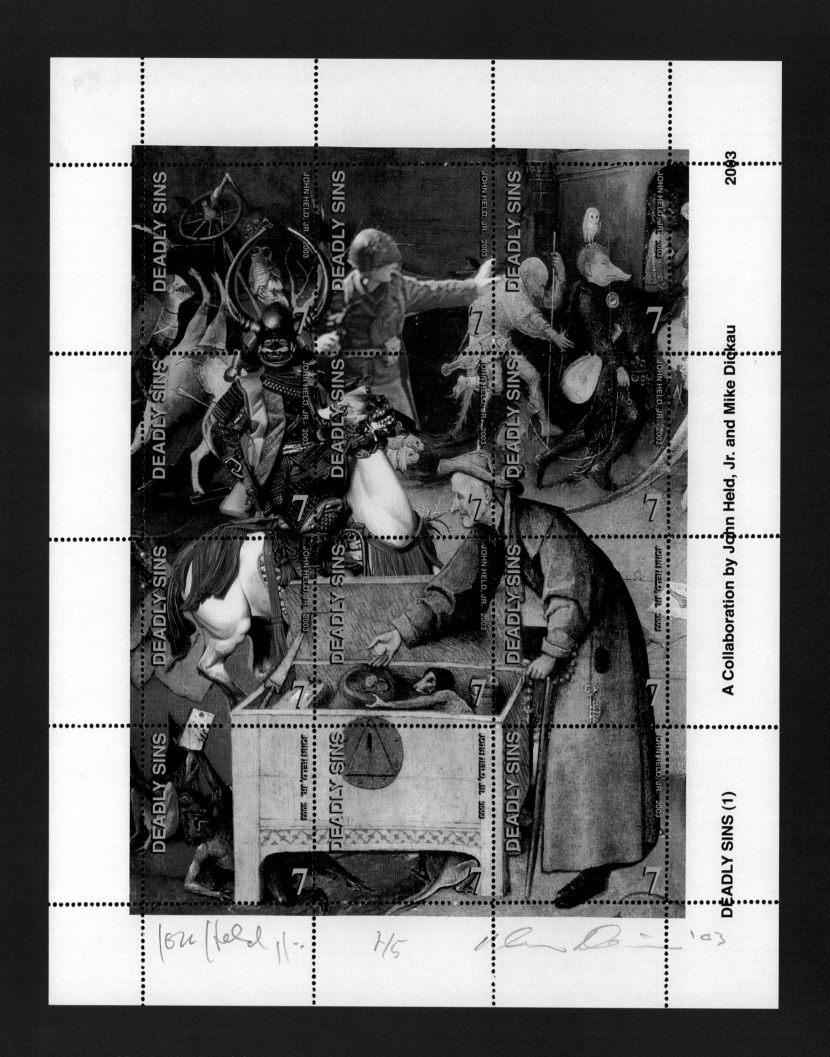

DEADLY SINS · 2003 · A Collaboration by John Held, Jr. and Mike Dickau · DEADLY SINS (1)

KARL SCHWESIG COMMEMORATIVE SHEET #1 by Jas. W. Felter

The original Artistamps by German artist Karl Schwesig (1898-1955) were drawn in colored ink on the blank perforated margins of an actual postage stamp sheet in Gurs, a large internment camp in unoccupied Vichy France and dated 'March, 1941.'

Reproduction rights to the Schwesig stamps courtesy of Galerie Remmert und Barth, Düsseldorf/West Germany; reproduction of the originals from the Collection of The Leo Beack Institute, New York. Published on the occasion of the INTERNATIONAL INVITATIONAL ARTISTAMP EXHIBITION, Dec. 7 - 31, 1989 by the Davidson Galleries, Seattle, Washington, USA.

Printed in Canada

Stamps produced by Banana Productions, Vancouver, Canada

The Angel

A WORLD MADE WORLD
A FLESH MADE WORLD
RAUSCH POST
A WORLD MADE FLESH

by **WARREN LEMING**

# of Evil

LUCIFER, THE ANGEL OF EVIL, WAS THE MOST BEAUTIFUL OF GOD'S ANGELS. *The Book of Common Prayer* warns us to beware of the Devil in all his allure. But Evil, the Seer from Hell, has a subtle attraction for humankind: it describes our condition without revealing its own.

Should we take time to consider what has happened, it waits to haunt us: Vietnam, El Salvador, Pinochet, the School of the Americas.

As a theological category, Evil curses our attempts at clarification. Having reduced the world to Good and Evil, the Theologians depart, leaving us the seared remnants of what used to be called Western Civilization.

Consider Berlin from the air in 1945. Block after block of Techno-perfected devastation. The smoking remains of the Reich's Chancellory are the first photo op in what was to become a perpetual War between Good and Evil.

Evil serves as the basis for all crime fiction. Its personifications—Gilles de Rais, Moriarity, Messalina, the Countess Bathory, Caligula, and the Borgias—rank with the greatest imaginative creations of world literature. No one looking at Goya's *Disasters of War* could deny that he has given Evil a human face.

Whole Federal Agencies lie in wait for it, funded by billions of taxpayer dollars. Homeland Security, with its murky blend of Fascism and apple pie platitude: "We must defeat Evil where we find it"—is another link in the long historical chain combating Evil. Combat the Axis of Evil? It's as if all the world's cliches had rallied around one concept.

Evil loves the secular, human form: whether the Hell Fire Club, or de Sade's raveups rife with failed sperm. The Devil appears in countless pieces of folk wisdom: Satan, Lucifer, Beelzebub, Old Nick, The Dark Angel, Mephistopheles, Lord of the Flies, The Evil One is Evil incarnate. His wisdom is clever, penetrating, and effective.

If Good comes from Above, we mortals live below where the Devil and Evil have their due. Evil remains the antidote to inflated piety.

It serves as the basis for both the horror story and the religious tract. Dracula and Saint Augustine, Aquinas and Sherlock Holmes, Jesus and Sam Spade are spiritual allies in the Battle for Good. Evil shadows the current battle to the death: Capitalism's effort to destroy Democracy.

The agents of Evil are everywhere. Walter Benjamin points out that every great work of Art conceals a crime. Just as Atget's photos of Paris document the site of the crime, so the ruins of a Spanish village bombed by Hitler's Condor Legion produce Picasso's *Guernica*.

Dickens's *Hard Times*, Da Vinci's corpses, Daumier's 19th Century London with its prostitution and slums suggest that Evil is the handmaiden of great Art .

> **The State has made Evil its friend, but it must be careful lest its friend turn and destroy it....who polices the police?**

The agents of Evil come in two forms: the conscious and the unconscious. But how then can Evil be defeated? If, as the theologians postulate, Evil is natural to Man, in stamping it out we eliminate a fundamental portion of the human psyche. At least the Inquisitions, in persecuting Evil, made sure that the patient died of the cure.

Bin Laden—like Stalin and Hitler before him—is the new poster child of Evil. But in having created him and attempting to destroy him, the State has made him a folk hero. Where once it was infamous, Evil is now famous. Pick the crime and create your own Pop Star.

Milton makes nothing of God, yet extends Lucifer's legend a thousand years. Romantic literature is one long testament to the dramatic life of Evil. Nietzsche insists that "All Romanticism ends in death." But Evil perfumes the coffin.

Whether *Jane Eyre* or *Crime and Punishment*, Byron or Baudelaire, World literature is one long hymn to the centrality of Evil. If War is the health of the State, Evil is its advertising.

Trotsky said: "All states are founded on violence," and what is violence but systematic Evil? Advertising, marketing, and sales campaigns are funded struggles to control human memory. Memory, for the powerless, is the form that vengeance takes.

Historical memory must be obliterated in favor of the State's memory of itself: Fascism, Communism, and Capitalism all agree.

Propaganda remains the root of all Evil, defined here as the State lying to itself. How is the State to live with its crimes unless it lies to itself? The first rule of any State is that the unofficial History be forgotten. Ours is no exception. We know nothing of our real Past. The Frontier reduced to Cowboys and Indians, not

DEADLY SINS
JOHN HELD, JR. 2003
7
DEADLY SINS
JOHN HELD, JR. 2003
7
DEADLY SINS
JOHN HELD, JR. 2003
7
DEADLY SINS
JOHN HELD, JR. 2003
7

штабспочта

0 MOM

2003

Legislatures and urban cultures purchased and systematically corrupted by the railroads and commercial interests.

The American Civil War is still seen as the resolution of the Slavery question. But the South, having lost the War, won the Peace. A Peace which saw the birth of the Klan and a Cotton Curtain which sealed the Southern states from Justice for over a hundred years. The battle for Civil Rights occurs a full century after Appomattox.

Music is driven by the struggle between Good and Evil: whether Wagnerian spectacle or the posturing adolescence of Heavy Metal. If banality is Evil, Schlock Rock pipes the way.

The 20th century artist has an ally in Evil. If it destroyed Pound, it may have saved Eliot. The founders of English Modernism—Pound, Eliot and Wyndam Lewis—remain in thrall to its power. Beware the artists who have come to save you: they preach from coffins.

D'Annunzio's hymns to Fascism, Marinetti's poetic glorification of War, or the Goering theater with Grundgens (on whom Klaus Mann based his *Mephisto* novel) at its head, remain icons of Evil.

Baudelaire's kinky urbanity fuses a hundred years later with Genet's admonition: "Crime is the highest form of sensuality." Evil is now commercially available as a perfume.

William Burroughs misanthropic spew now defines Outsider Art for an Academy hooked on excremental hyper-aestheticism. Little wonder the modern artist loathes politics. In a market dominated by corporate collectors passing as art patrons, politics is death to the fledgling career. Leni Riefenstahl, whose films made an icon of Hitler, said it again and again: "I'm not political, I'm an artist."

"Where Evil is…only Evil can fight it." What better motto for CIA headquarters.

A recent survey revealed that Fox News, if watched regularly, produces a mindset completely at odds with fact. The perfect corporate result has been achieved, not with the automobile or technology, but in a mindless bath of misinformation delivered by a Diane Sawyer or a Peter Jennings. The paid hacks of disinfotainment are now Stars, promoted 24/7 by a media bent on making "experts" of newsreaders, whose expertise goes no further than a Tele Prompter. The triumph of the hacks is now writ in stone.

The media's "legacy" has been confusion, passivity and Oprah-style confessional. Television has taken human memory and reworked it to the sad agendas at the heart of Capitalism. Self-centered help, sentimentality, false consciousness, and Shop or Die shows mingle to form growth industries. Evil has no sell-by date.

How then define Evil, when those in charge of the public memory work not to end it, but to shape it? We live in a Spin Doctor State. What else is Spin but a program of lies and disinformation in the service of the State? Where does the CIA's thirty billion dollar budget go, if not to disinform, corrupt, spin, and distort? Knowing all of that, the American public continues to support terror so long as it is directed elsewhere. When it comes home, as in the Letelier/Moffat murders or 9/11, the blowback is dismissed.

Buber points out that Evil is defined, biblically, as indecision. The inability to act. Kissinger, Pilate, and Christ all long for the Cup to pass from them. They remain frozen in the Garden at Gethsemane, waiting to act.

God has been telling the world for centuries that He does not exist. The World continues to outwit Him. Goodness is too often

> **Historical memory must be obliterated in favor of the State's memory of itself: Fascism, Communism, and Capitalism all agree.**

passive; Evil—active, alert, cunning. We are asked to choose from a long list of decisive indecisions. The human condition is unthinkable without Beelzebub as advisor. Evil is a form of human wisdom.

The ground under Evil is ever shifting and cyber savvy: today's friend, whether Saddam or Bin Laden or the Junta—is tomorrow's Evil. Today's Freedom Fighters, whether Nicaraguan Contra Army, McCarthyite hack, or Cointelpro twister—are revealed as a horror within a decade of their creation.

The State, the great agent of Crime in our Time, is never guilty. Each new discovery is, within months of its birth, corrupted to some abomination within the Governmental/Corporate agenda.

The computer begins as a means of calculating bomber combat kill statistics in World War Two. Think: Robert McNamara and Curtis "Let's bomb'em back to the Stone Age" Le May.

The State has made Evil its friend, but it must be careful lest its friend turn and destroy it. "If you create a police state, who polices the police?"

The State's definitions of Evil are ever shifting. The War against the Axis of Evil breeds Evil. We remain Triumphalists at a Wake, waving the tattered flags of a Victory that continues to defeat itself. Evil remains the greatest single historical force.

It drives the merchant as well as the artist. It is greed, the main chance, careerism, and illicit desire, which have forced the Past aside in a march to what we strangely call "the Future." All of Feudalism, Kingship, Aristocracy, and inherited privilege disappear as the Middle Classes begin their long march, spurred by technology and Kapital. Those in the palaces came to fear those in the huts. And if those in the huts did not come to rule, they

made the Rich fearful. We live with the well-advertised anxiety of millionaires posing as regular guys.

TV news programs breed a viral paranoia about people of color, the Poor, the disenfranchised. Corporate America looks at itself and calls for a Cop, or better yet, a Cop show. Sipowitz isn't just a thug with a badge: he's perpetual Fear posing as method Ham.

America's unease can be seen everywhere: from gated Greed Acres, where the white picket fence gives way to Security Guards with stun guns, to the bulletproofed limos waiting outside Gucci Gulch.

The automobile, machine gun and Carnegie's steel furnaces sweep away the old European order, and in its place comes something resembling modern America: vast shopping malls, the dismal suburban tract, a contentless system of misinformation and a bureaucratic order modeled on Vatican levels of indifference.

How to describe the wasteland now passing as "News, Fun and Prime Time"? Evil has been colorized and digitally jazzed for a new set of demographics.

Mussolini learned at the feet of the American philosopher William James, and Hitler's hero was the anti-Semite Henry Ford. Evil is nothing but the process through which history comprehends itself.

Technology has served to refine Evil and to perfect it. Science is Mephisto's best friend. We live in a century whose body count exceeds that of all the past ages combined. Evil is the category, essential to the mind of Man, through which Progress is promoted. Existence, like Evil, is steeped in paradox.

The Angel of Evil looks out over the chaos we call the World. The wind holding the Angel aloft has swept everything before it. This wind we call Progress. This wind we call History.

> **Where does the CIA's thirty billion dollar budget go, if not to disinform, corrupt, spin, and distort?**

48

DOO DA

STAMP MAKERS
ISSUE 2000

E.A.VIGO

VIGO

DOO DA

BOLIVIA

Michael H. De Lunes
AGENT
PROVACATURE
under the pay of
DICK CHANEY, &
ARIEL SHARON
(MOSBAD)
Says' to Stamp
Makers.....

43

WE GROW THESE IN TEXAS

FIRST CLASS

49

Al Gore is
ALL GORE

Jesse
Helms is
A MONSTER

Ross
Perot is
The MONEY

Bill Clinton is the
WRONGMAN

Newt Gingrich Is
The PHANTOM
OF the HOUSE

52

51

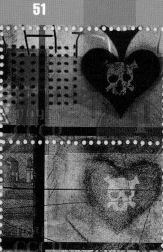

USA **37**

BLOOD FOR OIL

47

53

Assholes of

Arrogance

44

Woody Allen
Kosher Pedophile
incestuous geschlecht

"she had a virgin Kezele."

37
USA

ASS POST

46

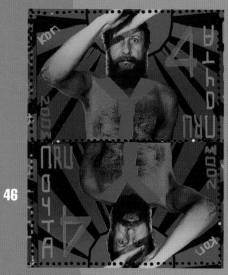

US

PATRIOT ACT 3

41

54

BLAME BLAME
GOD. GOD.
BLAME BLAME
GOD. GOD.

45

"God told me to strike

at al Qaeda and I

struck them, and then

he instructed me to

strike at Saddam,

which I did, and now

I am determined to

solve the problem

in the Middle East."

– GEORGE W. BUSH

42

RIEN

RIEN

RIEN

40

55

50

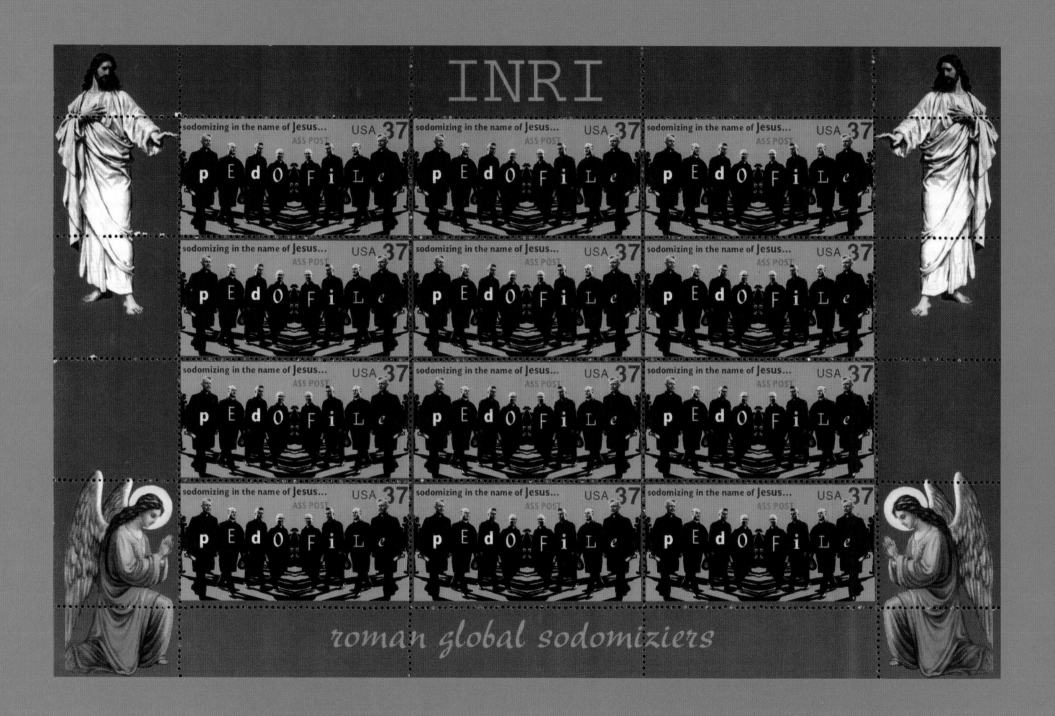

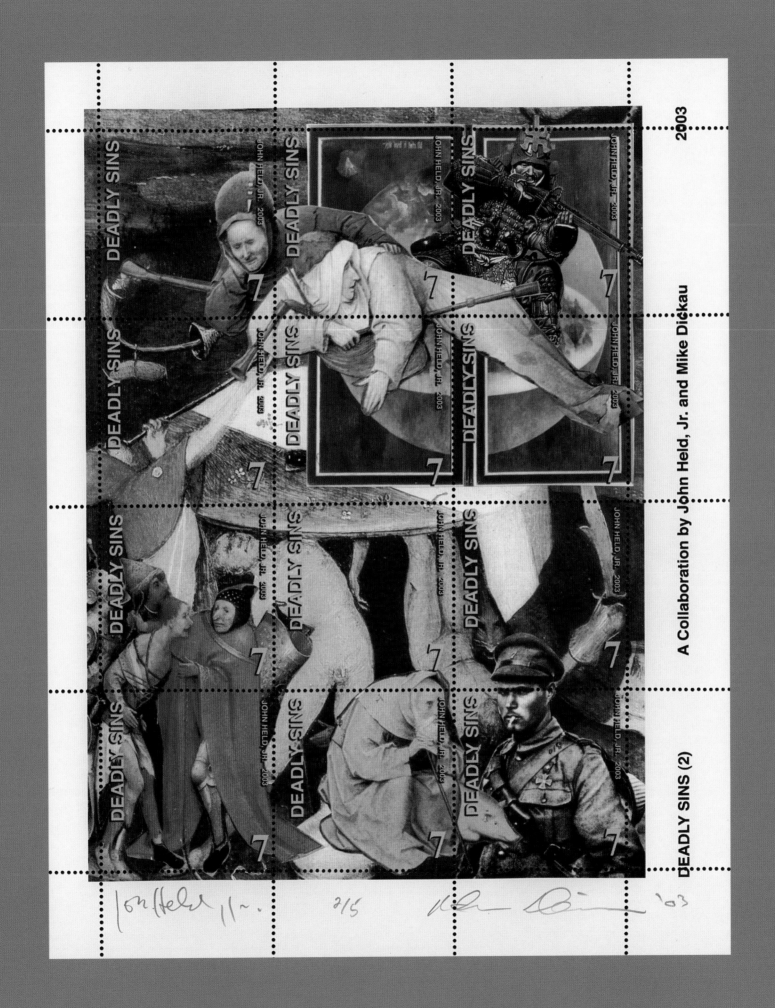

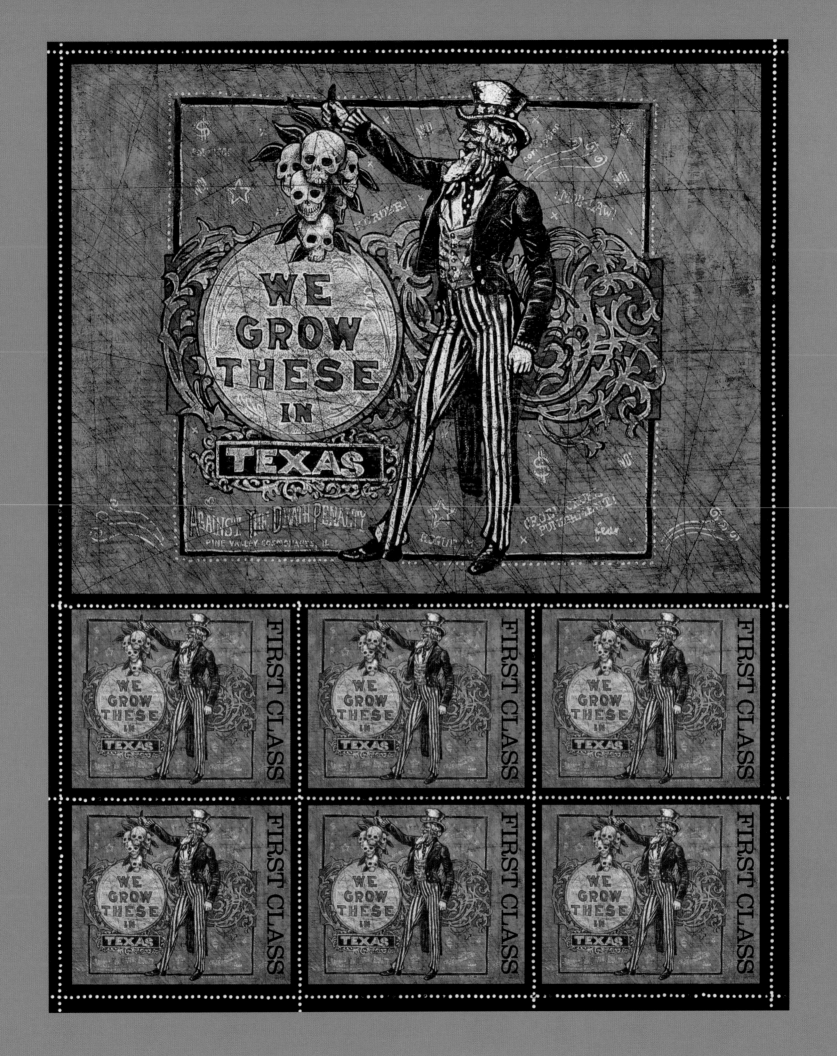

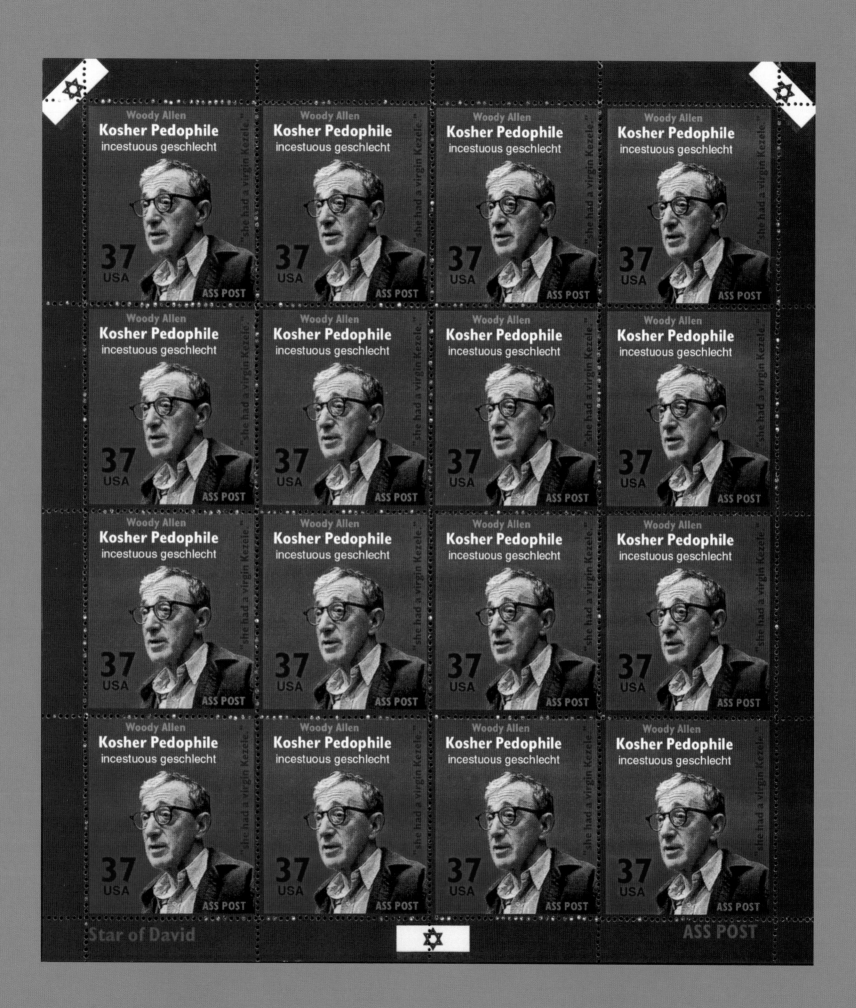

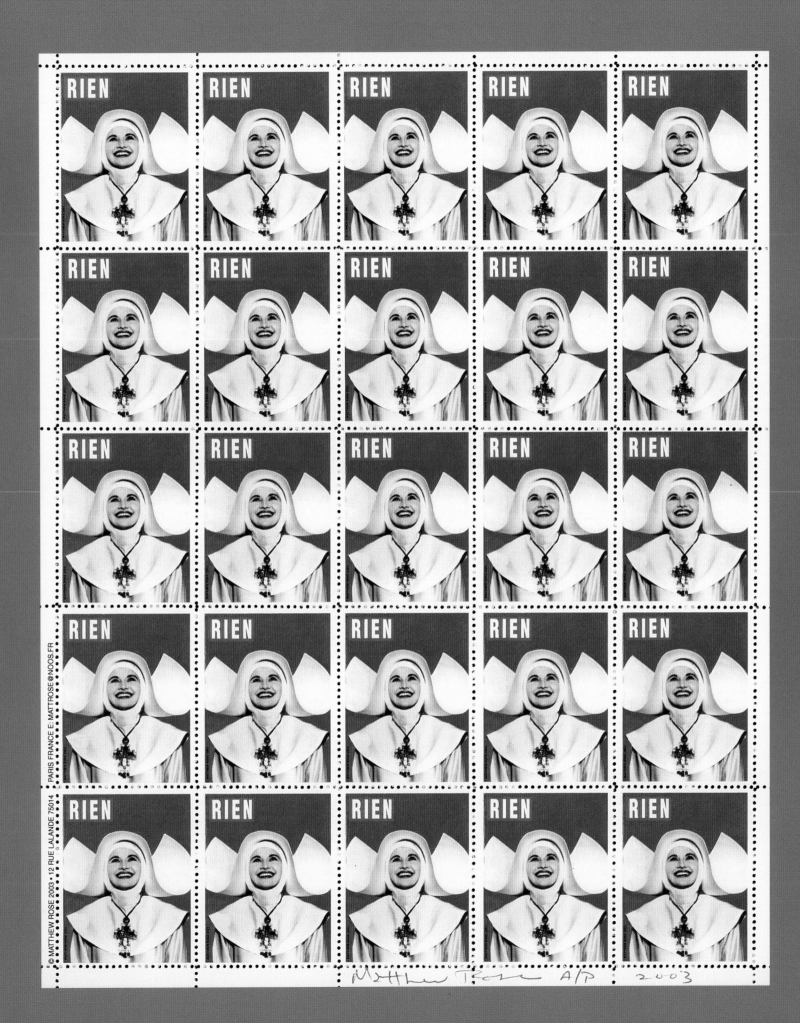

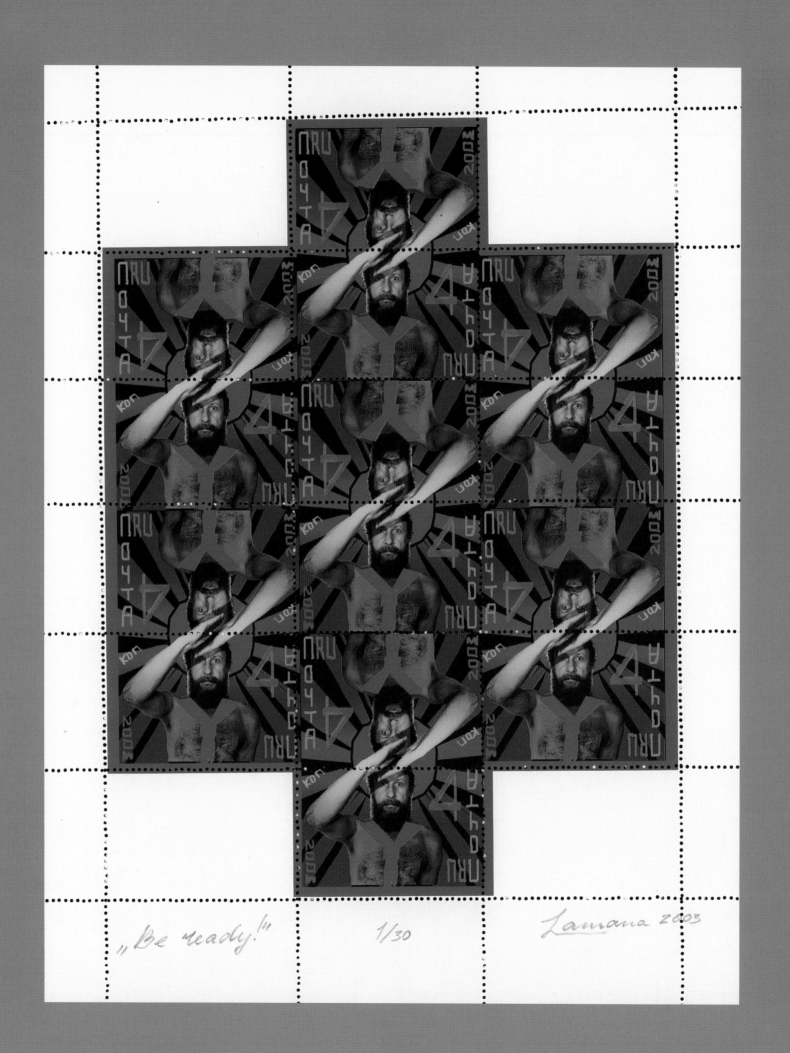

„Be ready!"   1/30   Lamana 2003

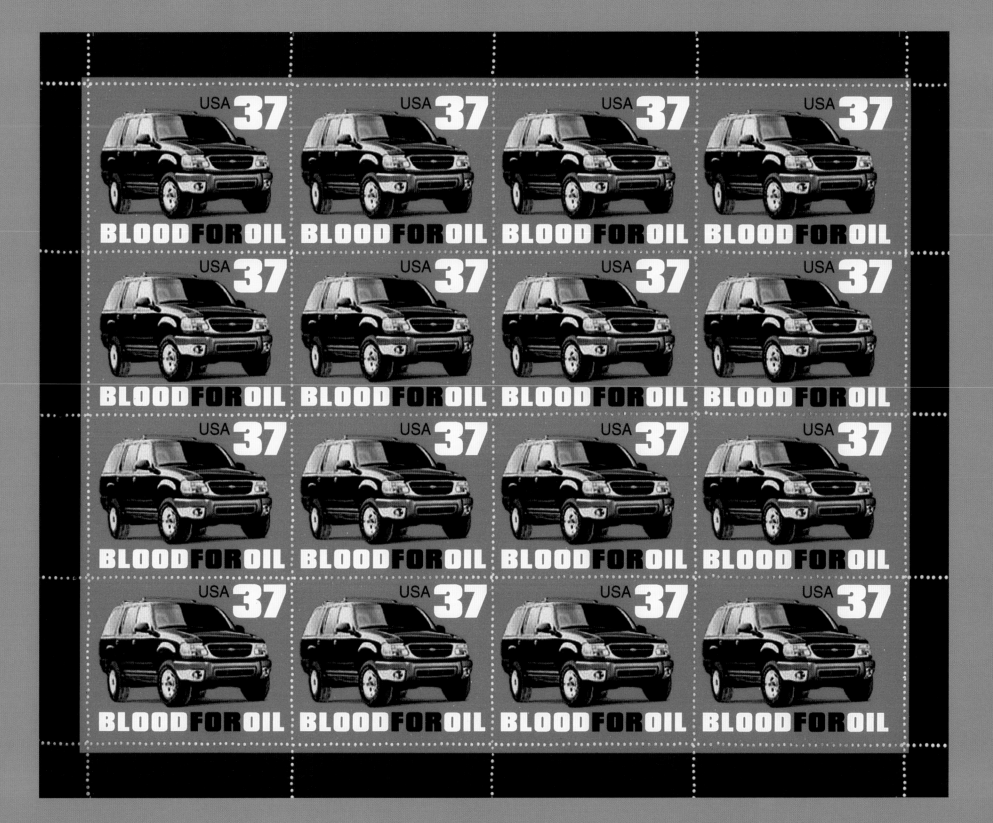

CONSPIRACY THEORY #312-MHDL #53
DOO DA
BOLIVIA
Michael H. De Lunes AGENT PROVACATURE under the pay of DICK CHANEY, & ARIEL SHARON (MOSSAD) Seys' to Stamp Makers....
COLUMBIA
ADMINISTRATION POSTALE DES NATIONS UNIES
GRAND PRIX DE L'ART PHILATELIQUE GROTE PRIJS VOOR FILATELISCHE KUNST
brussel bruxelles
BOYD'S CITY DISPATCH
2c.
E.A.VIGO
VIGO
HUMOR
RELIGON
SCREW BALL
Higgins Silhouette
Dear Mike, I fixed your right eye in the Photo., I don't know if this matters, but as a Painter, I think it looks better... Wadda ya think?
Michael Hernandez de Luna never trained at the Western Hemisphere Institute for Security Coooperation (WHINSEC) at Fort Bennings, Georgia.
693-*101803
Copyright 2003
LIES, MORE LIES, DUPLICITY, STUPIDITY, & GREED
A.P.
E.F. Higgins

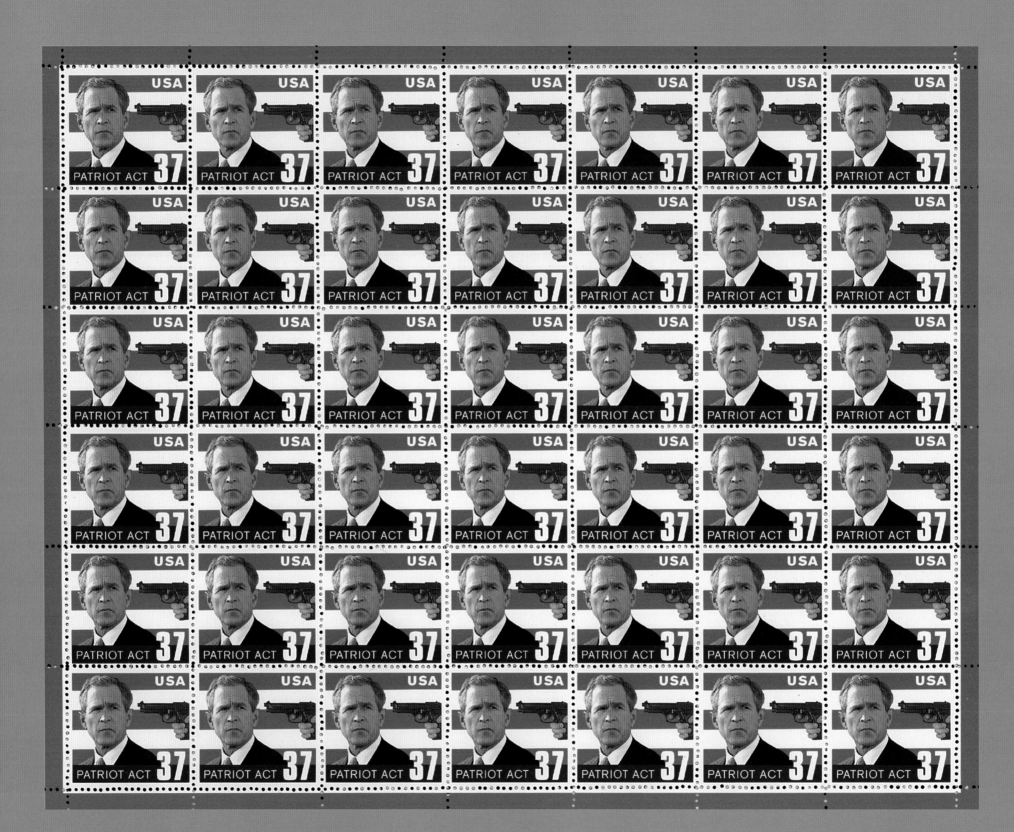

POST·NEO

ROCOLA

52 • Bela • **MARLON VITO PICASSO** • SAN LEANDRO-CALIFORNIA

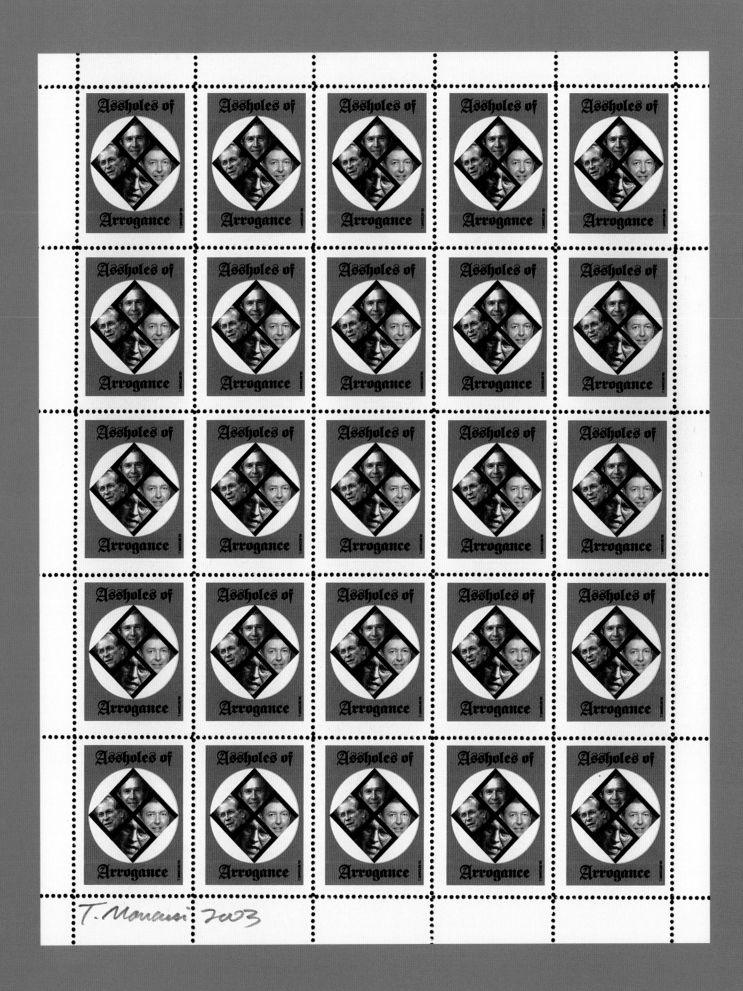

USGS-U.S. Geological Survey

A recent study by the Toxic Substances Hydrology Program of the USGS shows a broad range of chemicals found in residential, industrial, and agricultural wastewaters commonly occurs in mixtures at low concentrations downstream from intense urbanization and animal production. The chemicals included human and veterinary drugs(including antibiotics), natural and synthetic hormones, detergent metabolites, plasticizers, insecticides, and fire retardants...
Chemicals, used everyday in homes, industry and agriculture, can and do enter the environment in waste water.

So what's in that next glass, besides the water?

What is the impact on humans and our environment from this unseen chemical cocktail?

A glass of water?

Water &  bufo 04¢

03/08/04 maxwel A.P.

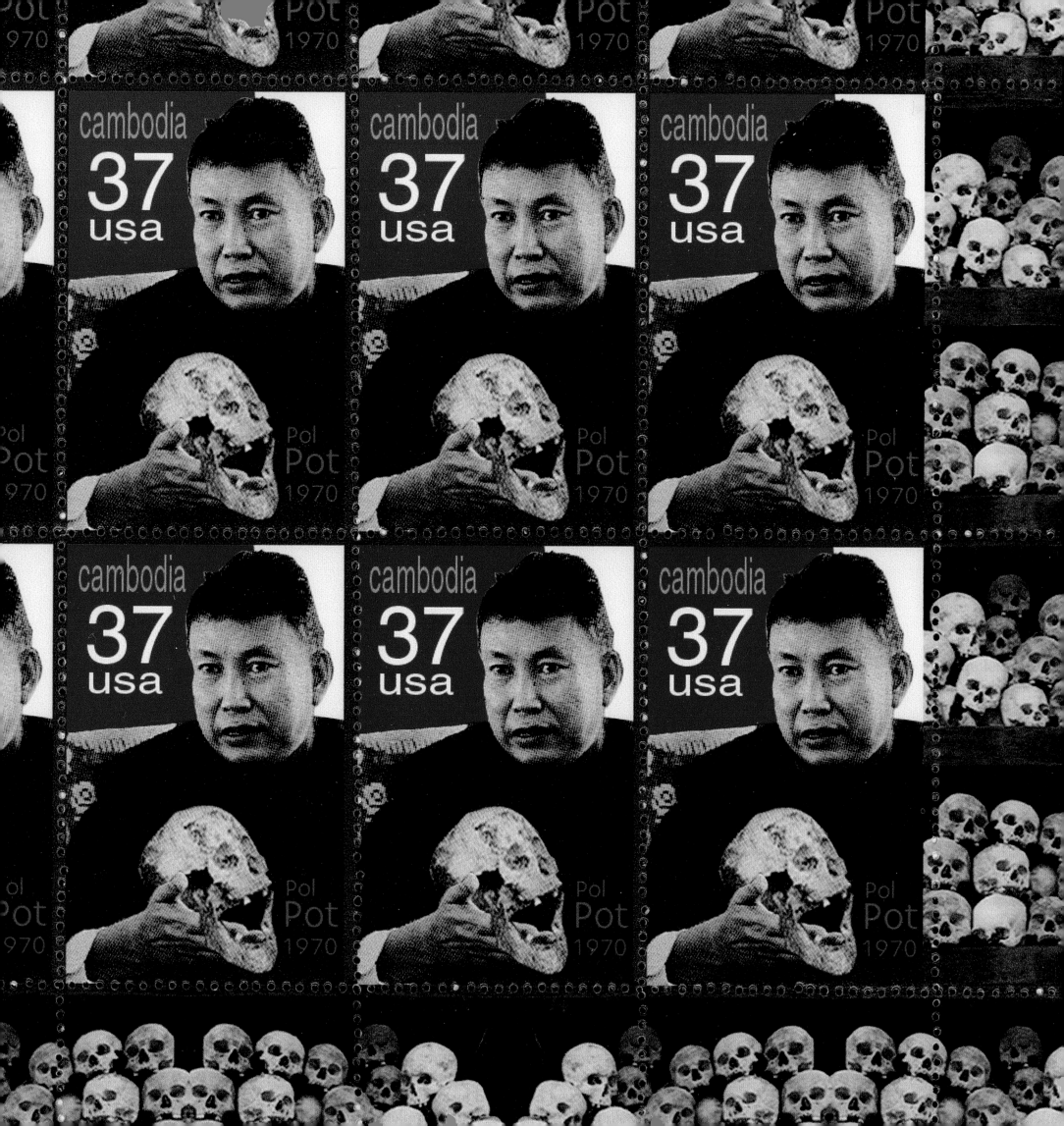

by DAVID BADE

ACCESS TO EVIL
oder
Adolf war ein Künstler seiner Zeit

So... you are off in search of evil?

EVERYBODY'S LOOKING FOR EVIL THESE DAYS: THE PRESIDENT OF THE UNITED STATES, the United States Congress, Army, and FBI, the German, Italian, French, Turkish, and Spanish police, and of course, Osama Bin Laden and Al-Qaeda, who find it in all of the above and in fact in all civilization outside the veil of Islam. But how to find evil?

For some, like Bin Laden, Noam Chomsky, and Communist Party members, evil *is* America; for the Moral Majority, PETA, Republicans, Democrats, and anti-Semites, evil is everywhere *within* America—but all these folks want to do is to get rid of it! The governments, armies, and police forces also want to get rid of evil, but for some reason they have a hard time finding it—it never shows up where it is supposed to, only where it isn't expected—and getting rid of it seems next to impossible, hampered as they often are in not-so-evil regimes by constitutions, human rights treaties, and an informed citizenry.

Then there are the librarians, who like to talk the talk but often balk at walking the walk, hampered as they are by a tremendous desire to reject censorship while at the same time appearing politically correct—whatever that may be at the moment—and these are clearly incompatible objectives. "Access!" they honk with their professional hats on, "Free access, to everything, everywhere, for everyone!" and sit back in their swivel chairs and dream of government monies and fresh young bodies filling their ranks. Then someone wants to read *Hustler* in the main reading room, a bearded man checks out *The Anarchist's Cookbook,* an ominously Muslim-looking woman wants a map of New York City, or a parolee requests a book kept in "special collections": *How to have sex with kids* (by the Howard Nichols Society; introduction by David Sonenschein). "They sell those across the street you know", is the icy reply to the first, and to the aged hippy and the lady, "Wouldn't you rather read *Walden,* young man?" and "How about a map of Havana instead?" while the parolee's request is referred to the Head Librarian who calls the patron into his office and asks "Wouldn't *Christopher Street* be more wholesome for men of our age, sir? Fabulous jacket! Italian? But really, those pants have GOT to go. ..."

Democracy, intellectual freedom, freedom of access to information—how could a modern library survive without these? After all, apart from the teachings of a few religious fanatics and their millions of followers around the world, totalitarian regimes with their rigid control of information and censorship are things of the past, even for the most progressive members of the Left! What academic library could do without the *Communist Manifesto,* the *Protocols of the Elders of Zion, Mein Kampf,* and all those other works of such great historic importance, the speeches and writings of sadistic, power-worshipping, money-grubbing, ass-kissing intellectuals and dictators from Sorel to Mao, Nietzsche to Trotsky, Engels to Lenin, Lukacs to Stalin, Schmitt to Mussolini, Sombart to Fish, Riefenstahl to Brecht, Sartre to Pol Pot, Solanas to MacKinnon, Celine to Pauline, Cioran to Ceaucescu, Friedmann to Foucault, Marcuse to Milosevic, the learned justifications and aesthetic celebrations of class, ethnic, religious, and sexist hatreds as well as cruelty to animals, that vast literature which incited hundreds of thousands to slaughter hundreds of millions of human beings (not to mention the animals!) in less than a century and continues to fascinate intellectuals and artists right up to the present day? Who could study 20th-century civilization anywhere in the world without reference to these fundamental texts of modern society, these master works of the evil imagination? Who needs to consult churches, religion, and sacred texts concerning evil when you have masters such as these right at your fingertips in the library? Yet what better records exist for the study of evil than those ancient and sacred texts: Homer, the Bible, the Koran, the Mahabharata ... in which all manner of horrendous crimes are described, commanded by some deity or committed in his name?

Librarians can often get off the hook by telling the evil-minded reader, "That book is lost" or "Budget constraints prevent us from subscribing to *Snuff film quarterly*" or even "Sorry, but the Supreme Court's interpretation of the separation of church and state prohibits etc. etc." Still, it remains a difficult balancing act to oppose censorship, preach intellectual freedom and still manage to keep the public ignorant of the history of political, scientific, and religious ideologies of hatred, racism, sexism, and such primitive and harmful ideas as "Love your neighbor as yourself."

For all those of us who are looking for evil out there in the world, whether in books, movies, or on the World Wide Web, there always seem to be obstacles thrown in our paths, always someone who says, "No ma'am, that is not fit material for a nice girl like you" or who slaps a pair of cuffs on the brave revolutionary's wrists and hauls her off to jail for having violated some law against possession of hate literature, a Bible, a Koran, or "dirty-bomb" making manuals.

Yet there is one group of people who cannot be stopped, for they have discovered the most direct access to evil in all its forms, for whom no evil can be denied: the artist. The one great fact of the 20th century, what every one shudders to consider:

and those who do stamp their feet and scream their denial—all to no avail—for the truth is too well known: Hitler was an artist. Mao was a poet. This is a matter of the utmost importance, a key to the 20th century which everyone wants to forget, to deny, and to obliterate from human memory.

Hitler was an artist, the first—perhaps the greatest—performance artist, the first to realize personally and world-historically the full potential of the artist's access to evil. Bacon and Dali stuck to canvas; Mark Pauline is an amateur. Hitler alone has shown the full extent of the power of art to transform the world in which we live. The artist's terrible power is in his access to evil.

One need only look within, set the imagination free, hold nothing back, and one can find an inexhaustible fund of evil in one's own eager and willing soul. "The Kingdom of God is within you," Jesus proclaimed; the artist discovers that "The Kingdom of Evil is within you" and what productivity follows from that discovery! Who needs the world and hell when the Flower of Evil blossoms within you? The Artist creates Hell; he has no need to search for it, no need of the library.

If only we could understand what the artists discovered (or was it the Hebrew prophets?): if you are looking for evil, look within. As Solzhenitsyn wrote:

> If only there were evil people somewhere, insidiously committing evil deeds, and it were necessary only to separate them from the rest of us and destroy them. But the line dividing good and evil cuts through the heart of every human being. And who is willing to destroy a piece of his own heart?

So… look no further, my friends. THE AXIS OF EVIL IS WITHIN YOU, the truth will set you free!

65

IN STARTLING COLOR

PLAGUE OF THE ART

ZOMBIES

'X'

74

SLUT-HOLE 66 USA

MOTHERFUCKER 66 USA

NUT 66 USA

70

Hamas Baby Bomb

37 usa

75

IOCK & AWE NAW

BAGHDAD

68

COW TOWN ART

SMOKING POSTAGE 10

COW TOWN ART

SMOKING POSTAGE 10

62

77

Freedom from

Imprisonment

$

USA 33

67

MOSCOW, RUSSIA

STEEL HAND & PETROV POSTAGE

2000 К ДЕКАБРЬ

MOSCOW, RUSSIA

STEEL HAND & PETROV POSTAGE

2000 К ДЕКАБРЬ

71

GLOBAL MAIL

1996

peace

pwb post

76

73

66

64

69

63

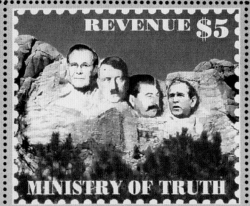

72

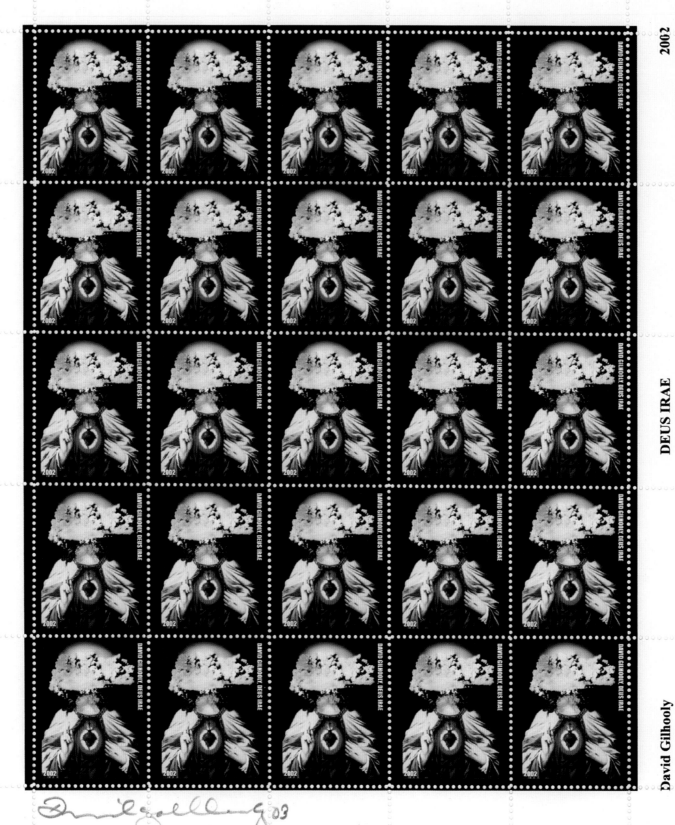

2002

DEUS IRAE

David Gilhooly

Back to Paradise • IVAN KOLENIKOV / SERGEJ DENISOV WITH VASILILIJ BOGATCHOV / PAVEL KISELJOV / JAMIYA YASINSKAYA • MOSCOW-RUSSIA

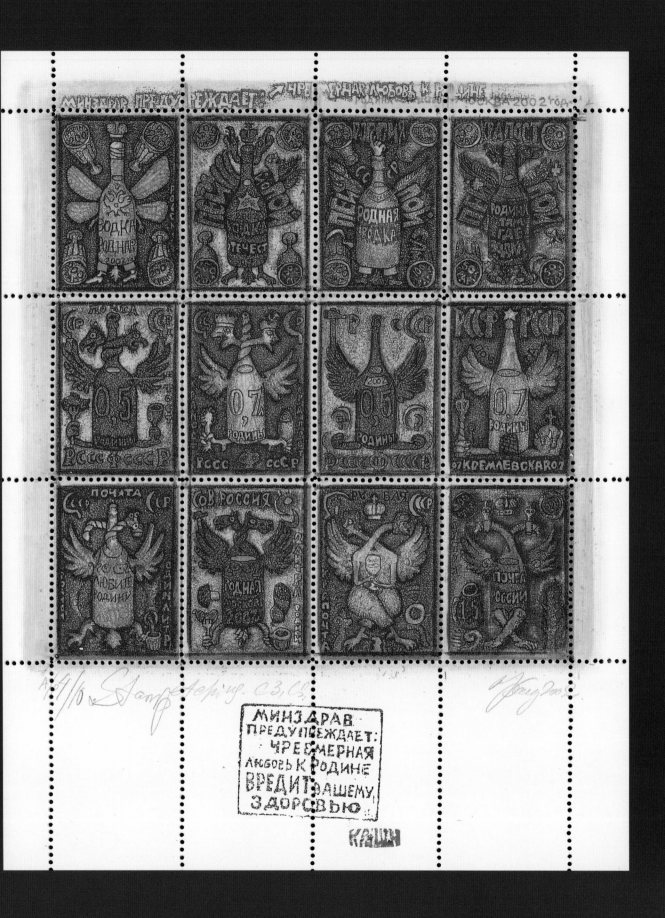

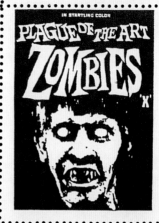

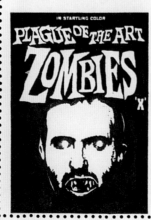

VITTORE BARONI FOR STRANGE CORRESPONDENCES™ '89 · COPY N.100

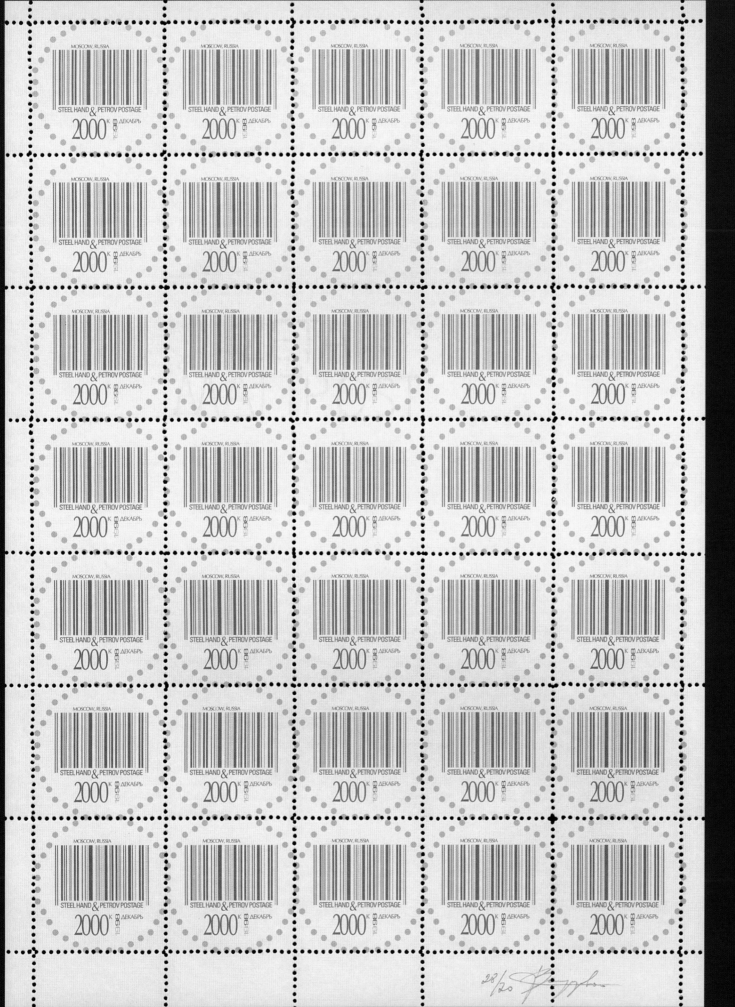

28/20

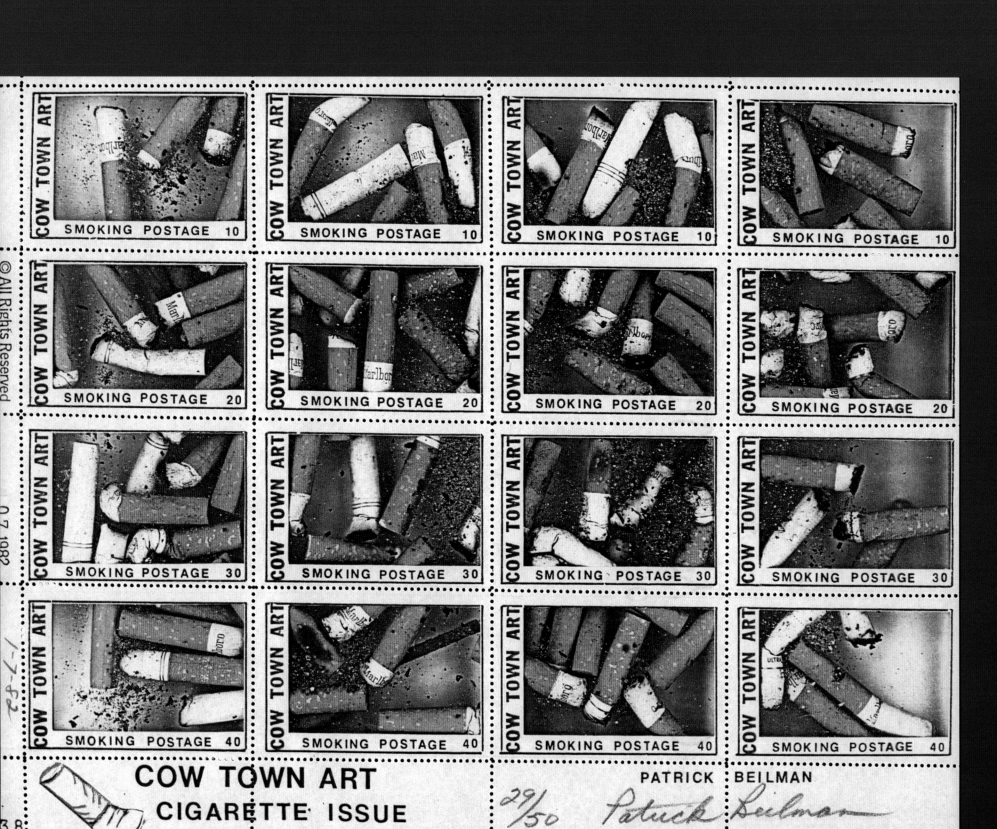

COW TOWN ART
CIGARETTE ISSUE

PATRICK BEILMAN

29/50

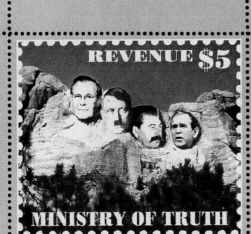

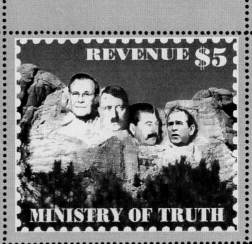

HARLEY (American 1940-) 2003

• Hamas Baby Bomber • **MICHAEL HERNANDEZ DE LUNA** • CHICAGO-ILLINOIS

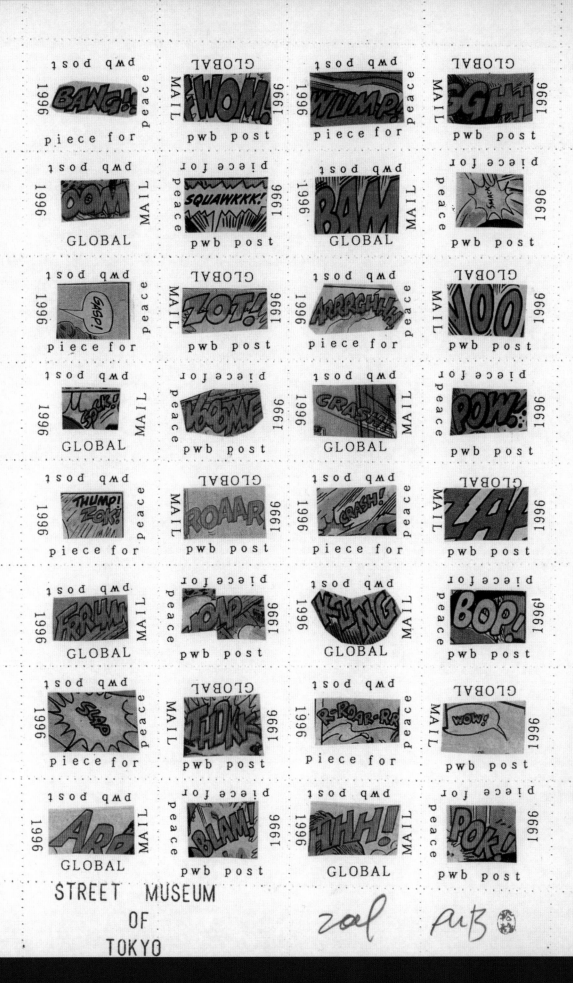

ONE DIETH IN — JOEL SMITH COMMEMORATIVE PLAGUE

HIS FULL STR — JOEL SMITH COMMEMORATIVE PLAGUE

ENGTH BEING — JOEL SMITH COMMEMORATIVE PLAGUE

WHOLLY AT E — JOEL SMITH COMMEMORATIVE PLAGUE

ASE AND QUIE — JOEL SMITH COMMEMORATIVE PLAGUE

T HIS BREAST — JOEL SMITH COMMEMORATIVE PLAGUE

S ARE FULL — JOEL SMITH COMMEMORATIVE PLAGUE

OF MILK AND — JOEL SMITH COMMEMORATIVE PLAGUE

HIS BONES A — JOEL SMITH COMMEMORATIVE PLAGUE

RE MOISTENE — JOEL SMITH COMMEMORATIVE PLAGUE

D WITH MARR — JOEL SMITH COMMEMORATIVE PLAGUE

OW AND ANOT — JOEL SMITH COMMEMORATIVE PLAGUE

HER DIETH IN — JOEL SMITH COMMEMORATIVE PLAGUE

THE BITTERN — JOEL SMITH COMMEMORATIVE PLAGUE

ESS OF HIS SO — JOEL SMITH COMMEMORATIVE PLAGUE

UL AND NEVE — JOEL SMITH COMMEMORATIVE PLAGUE

R EATETH W — JOEL SMITH COMMEMORATIVE PLAGUE

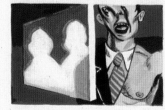
ITH PLEASU — JOEL SMITH COMMEMORATIVE PLAGUE

RE THEY SH — JOEL SMITH COMMEMORATIVE PLAGUE

ALL LIE DOWN — JOEL SMITH COMMEMORATIVE PLAGUE

ALIKE IN THE — JOEL SMITH COMMEMORATIVE PLAGUE

DUST AND THE — JOEL SMITH COMMEMORATIVE PLAGUE

WORMS SHA — JOEL SMITH COMMEMORATIVE PLAGUE

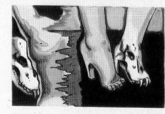
LL COVER TH — JOEL SMITH COMMEMORATIVE PLAGUE

EM BEHOLD I — JOEL SMITH COMMEMORATIVE PLAGUE

Joel Smith   16/200   Jcb

"FULCRUM"

WEEF-01-02-04-07-03-55-UK

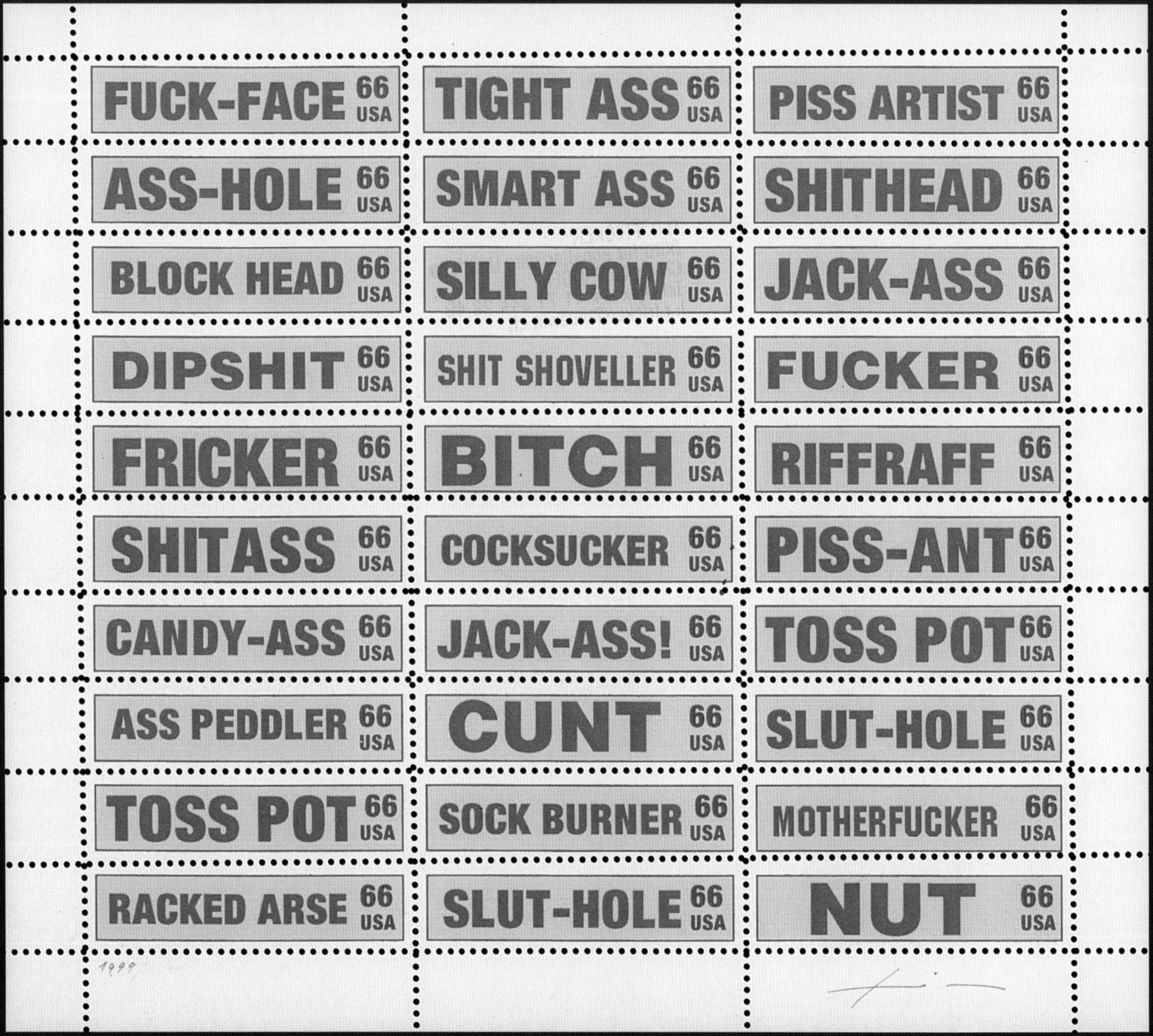

74 • Untitled • **HR FRICKER** • TROGEN-SWITZERLAND

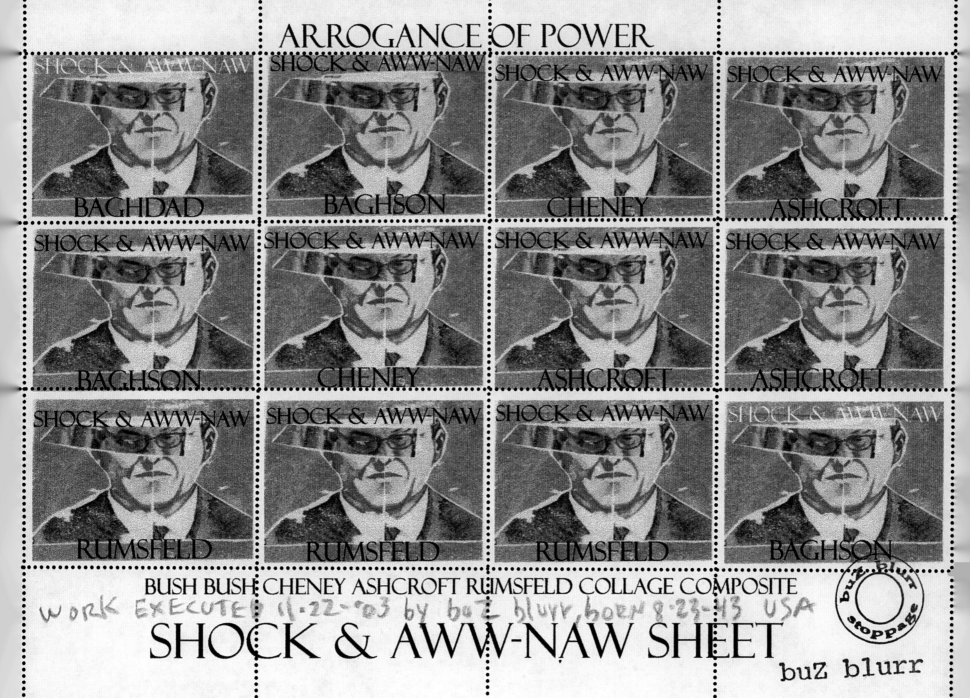

ARROGANCE OF POWER

SHOCK & AWW-NAW
BAGHDAD

SHOCK & AWW-NAW
BAGHSON

SHOCK & AWW-NAW
CHENEY

SHOCK & AWW-NAW
ASHCROFT

SHOCK & AWW-NAW
BAGHSON

SHOCK & AWW-NAW
CHENEY

SHOCK & AWW-NAW
ASHCROFT

SHOCK & AWW-NAW
ASHCROFT

SHOCK & AWW-NAW
RUMSFELD

SHOCK & AWW-NAW
RUMSFELD

SHOCK & AWW-NAW
RUMSFELD

SHOCK & AWW-NAW
BAGHSON

BUSH BUSH CHENEY ASHCROFT RUMSFELD COLLAGE COMPOSITE

WORK EXECUTED 11-22-'03 by buz blurr, born 8-23-43 USA

SHOCK & AWW-NAW SHEET

buz blurr stoppage

buz blurr

buz blurr

Have

USA

Nada

Have not

Freedom from

Imprisonment

$

USA 33

33 USA

Slave to

Empowerment

$

Forget

The High Life

U$A

forever   broke

Who's Bitch

ARMS OF EVIL

by RENAY KERKMA

EVIL HOLDS SPECIAL CONNECTIONS TO THE WORLD of childhood. As children, we feel safe when held in our parents' warm arms; we feel scared if a stranger grabs us. In the past, naughty children were told bedtime stories of evil—fairy tales based on historical figures—to scare them into blind obedience and sleep. To warn children about danger and cruelty, shocking parables describe evil people and evil itself as a noun. Rebellious teenagers doubt their parents' warnings, get disgusted by shameless media manipulation, and mock the traditional stories of evil. Evil becomes a joke—dark pubescent humor transgressing taboos. Eighties punk rock embraced psychopathic figures in songs, mass murderer playing cards, and stories that demonstrated the extremes of evil that people can execute or become. A favorite serial killer story was of Gilles de Rais: an evil aristocrat, a military hero, and a comrade of Joan of Arc.

As military chief of staff and a nobleman of 15th century France, Gilles de Rais was above the law. Peasant children were enticed to his castle by a woman known as "La Meffraye" (the Terror). He wrapped his arms around the peasant children, hugged them, pampered them, fed them, dressed them up in fancy clothes, caressed them, led them upstairs, hung them from hooks, sodomized them, and then hugged, kissed, and carved their dead bodies—admiring their headlessness, sliced inner organs, and tender limbs. A rumor circulated that Gilles enjoyed sitting on the stomachs of dying children, practicing witchcraft, and masturbating. Over the 14 years of Gilles' alleged debauchery, more than 140 peasant children disappeared but were not genuinely missed (small and poverty-stricken human life was cheap); not until an adult clergyman was murdered was Gilles de Rais arrested. As Terror and Evil go walking hand in hand, childhood nightmares can be triggered years later, in the event of large-scale horror, to summon adult panic. Nations take up arms to kill Evil; the most obvious material for cannon fodder becomes the flesh of small children.

When I was five years old, an evil man with retractable accordion-spring arms lived under my bed. He had a special counterpart: darkness. His expandable mechanical arms were cast with every sunset; every morning at daybreak the metal man died —melting away in a mysterious foundry of light. At nightfall, my bed became a little prison of mechanical shadows. Arms of Evil huddled below, groping and piercing the air with cold metal vapors. I could feel his presence as if it were an electrical force buzzing below me. Terrorized by the darkness, I was forced to stand in the middle of the bed and jump to the farthest point by the

> When I was five years old, an evil man with retractable accordion-spring arms lived under my bed.

doorway — for some odd reason the doorway was a safe zone—to avoid the grasp of his evil telescopic arms. Sometimes he made an appearance in my dreams; however, unlike the physical laws that I had created for my bedroom, in dreams I could always fly away. His face was a diamond-shaped wad of angles, green metal skin, and black beady dots for eyes—eyes different than mine that could see through the darkness. Arms of Evil wore only a sinister grin. Emerging with menacing smirks from a manhole that appeared only at night, he existed solely to grab my ankles and yank me into his mechanical hell. If I should die

before I wake, I pray the Lord my soul to take.

Ashamed of my own imagination, I told no one, seeking solace in Bible School stories. Unfortunately, many of the stories from my Methodist Bible School storybooks were based on acts of filicide and tales of human sacrifice. The histories of our invisible and singular God—for some strange reason—highlight an episode circa 2100 B.C. to 1500 B.C. when a man named Abraham got the homicidal idea from somewhere (God, Satan, or his own psychopathic delusions) that he should butcher his son (Isaac or Ishmael depending on whether your version of the story is Christian, Jewish, or Islamic) with a knife as a blood sacrifice to God. To a child, this story is terrifying. Had Abraham gone through with the order, he would have then burnt the flesh of his son as an offering. Claiming bloodline property rights over desert lands, descendants of Abraham continue to tell this story; the sands continue to soak up the blood of his rival descendants. If one of our parents lies to us, beats us, has sex with us, or drowns us in the bathtub, we learn the meaning of betrayal. Betrayal complicates evil; the arms that we run to for comfort could be a pedophile, a rapist, or a murderer. In the tradition of sacrificial son killing, boys march off to war and the Christian God so

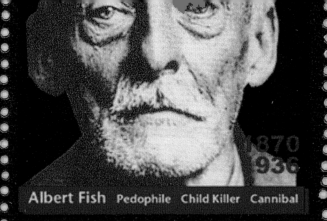

1928

1870
1936

Albert Fish Pedophile Child Killer Cannibal

1927

Bl

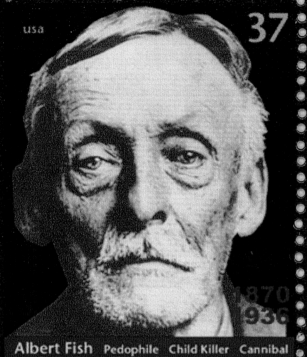

usa 37

usa 37

usa 37

1870
936

1870
936

1870
936

Albert Fish Pedophile Child Killer Cannibal

Albert Fish Pedophile Child Killer Cannibal

Albert Fish Pedophile Child Killer Cannibal

usa 37

1870
1936

Albert Fish Pedophile Child Killer Cannibal

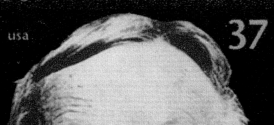

usa 37

7

Kill

Eat

A Fan of Charles Manson

A Fan of Peter Kürten

A Fan of Mark Chapman

THE ART VILLAGE · IDIOT · POST

1
A Fan of Myra Hindley

POST · IDIOT · THE ART VILLAGE

1
A Fan of Albert DeSalvo

POST · IDIOT · THE ART VILLAGE

1
A Fan of Graham Young

POST · IDIOT · THE ART VILLAGE

1
A Fan of Ed Gein

POST · IDIOT · THE ART VILLAGE

1
A Fan of Ted Bundy

POST · IDIOT · THE ART VILLAGE

1
A Fan of George W. Bush

loved the world that he gave his only begotten Son. Lead us not into temptation, but deliver us from evil.

After studying religious stories in Bible School, my fears of the Arm of Evil under my bed was compounded by a sacral knowledge that sometimes parents are told by God to kill their children. One sunny summer day I was playing on the floor of my room with fashion dolls and pieces of an Erector Set when I started to smell something very, very stinky. I ran and told my mother who solved the problem by opening my window. I was outside riding my tricycle for a while and then returned to playing with my toys on the floor of my room. A big fuzzy tail suddenly swished out from beneath the bed. Curious, I peeked behind the bedspread to find a big German shepherd crouched in the corner—smashed flat, hiding, and panting away with a slobbering tongue and big teeth. Like a desperate wolf, he looked scared and hungry and he smelled like a skunk. He was a vicious guard dog normally kept on a short leash with a muzzle, used by our neighbors to guard a construction supply yard. I ran and told my mother that there was a big wolf under my bed and that he was hungry. She laughed and gave me a piece of bread to feed him.

I lay flat besides him and gave him little pieces of the bread slice. This went on for two hours—I would run to the kitchen and get more and more bread for my new friend the vicious junkyard dog. Finally, my mother came in to see what was happening to the entire loaf of bread. She screamed in horror, grabbed me by my arm and pulled me out to the living room, slamming the bedroom door. The police came with guns and nets. The owner of the dog came with the short leash and the muzzle and big apologies to my parents. I was a little sad to see him go, and was never scared of the evil man under my bed again. Apparently, the dog was so hungry that he had eaten the

> ## War is a series of acts involving gallant butchery; murder in peacetime is an evil taboo.

man with mechanical arms, sealing off the manhole to hell forever.

Conjuring up fears of absolute yet ethereal evil is an effective instrument in the control of children, religious devotees, and nations going to war. God is all good; the devil is all evil. Gory representations of a crucified Son decorate Catholic churches and Hollywood movies; sons full of bloody nails come back to haunt us in coffins covered with flags. During times of war, we unite the love of God and the love of country with the sacrificial son ritual: heroic acts of patriots. War is a series of acts involving gallant butchery; murder in peacetime is an evil taboo. Forbidden, unthinkable acts that result in the rural carnage left by mass murderers such as Ed Gein shock the peaceable countryside. How could anyone not know the difference between eating venison and subsequently decorating with the taxidermy of deer, and eating people and subsequently decorating with the taxidermy of humans? Where did he cross the line?

The nipple belts, the skull teacups, the three piece suit of human skin represent one of the most sensational and foul artifacts to make front-page news; decades later Gein becomes the bases of *Psycho*, *The Texas Chainsaw Massacre* and countless other Hollywood and punk rock anthems of shock and horror. Evil becomes a star on a deck of serial killer playing cards. We search for explanations. He was evil. He was crazy. He was evil and crazy. Discussing how the crazy, evil Ed Gein spent his remaining years on a psych ward, I am sitting in a rural roadside tavern asking the bartender if she has ever heard the song, "Nipple Belt." A smartly dressed elderly man at the bar interrupts the conversation: "Oh, the butcher of Plainfield." He goes on to say that he worked on that psych ward as a psychologist and that he had known Ed very well. Ed was a very pleasant man. I inquire of the man claiming Gein expertise what the diagnosis was. He says, "Well—psychopath, of course." I then ask, "Did Ed ever show any remorse?" "No," replied the shrink, "He was proud of his work. He was a craftsman."

Professionals engaged in the field of Abnormal Psychology study sadistic and violent human behavior. Psychoanalysis was a shunned profession until they found it helpful in Germany after the First World War. The "devil's paintbrush" (a catchy name given the newly perfected WWI machine gun) mixed with trench warfare, air bombing, and gas left crazed WWI soldiers shocked from shells. Mental hospitals filled to the brim. Soldiers needed a quick fix for reprogramming so that they could be sent back into the battlefields. Brutality that would be unimaginable in peacetime is expected of the soldier as standard labor. A soldier is a craftsman of death via blind obedience. While the sensitive shell-shocked soldier is hunted down by the demons of war, the psychopath is proud of his work. He lacks empathy—either from military training in the coldhearted approach to killing, or he brings along with him to military enlistment that businesslike, matter-of-fact deadness.

The death of empathy is sad; however, the failure to ever develop any empathy as a child is heartbreaking and dangerous. At the age of two, children engage in parallel play and have no understanding that they should not hurt people. A two-year-old named Joey ran into a room where I lay unsuspectingly on the floor. He shattered my face with the back of his head and screamed, "Smash face—ha, ha," and ran away. He felt no remorse. As an avid hockey fan, his father had taught him to play the "smash-face" game. My nose was broken and I was in a great deal of pain for months. His parents took no responsibility for his actions. They both ended up in ankle bracelets with electronic ties to the

> ...the failure to ever develop any empathy as a child is heartbreaking and dangerous.

police—sociopathic criminals stealing people's identities for a living. Joey now takes speed for his ADHD; he sits in a chair watching Tom and Jerry smash each other in the face. Perhaps someday he will become a CEO for a company hell-bent on war profiteering. Lacking compassion is very helpful in big business. Joey may never feel sympathy; he may never feel anything outside of himself. If anyone changes the animation channel or lowers the sound, he screams and panics as if the soundtracks of cartoons keep his demons away.

Devil spirits haunt children, soldiers disturbed by gory military lunacy, and the religious. As a fundamentalist Christian, I was saved from my wayward teenage years to find myself plagued by clouds of evil that followed me everywhere. Although I did like the idea of speaking in tongues—acquiring the ability to speak numerous languages with no study or understanding of what I was saying—I was inundated with thoughts of the devil.

Embracing beliefs of being stalked by evil tends to handicap a person with a constant and vague foreboding. Fifteenth-century retablas erupt through the ground from hell around every corner, they flash arms with pointing claws reaching out of the earth with one brilliant demon swinging from the trees adorned with multiple sinister grins—faces on his stomach, buttocks, chest—reaching down with claws for the heads of pious clergy. Paralyzed by evil forces, I found the escape from evil to be through atheism. However boring atheism seems, it can always be augmented with the belief in a simple force that is God, philosophy, quantum physics, spiritual quests, and a love for the human race. Miraculously, the demons and the arms of evil departed at the precise moment that I ceased to be religious. Now, I am free to worry about the sudden appearance of men armed with the devil's paintbrushes, war profiteers, and vicious dogs.

99

102

92

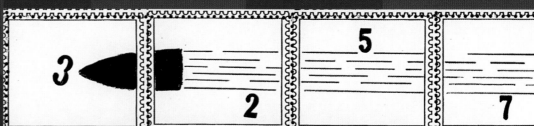

95

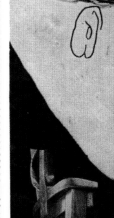

90

8

5

97

91

93

napalm 37

Vietnam

98

"Hustlers of the world, there is one Mark you cannot beat. The Mark inside....Exterminate all rational thought."
— WILLIAM S. BURROUGHS

104

106

94

103

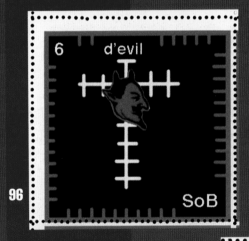

Urban Adventures USA

100

USA boys 666

1

6   d'evil

SoB

96

101

| USA 10 | USA 10 | USA 10 |
| @ | $ | ONLY SENDERS CAN BE LOCATED |

5   5

88

89

COLLATERAL DAMAGE   COLLATERAL DAMAGE   COLLATERAL DAMAGE   COLLATERAL DAMAGE

USA 37   USA 37   USA 37   USA 37

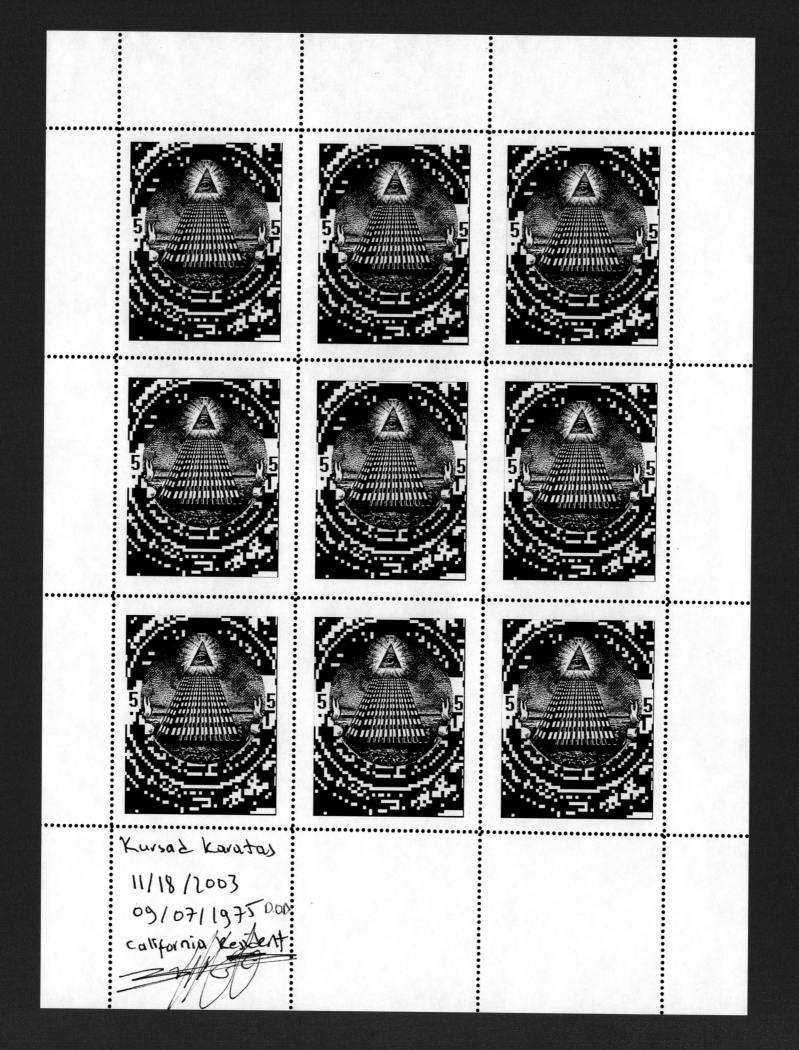

Kursad Karatas
11/18/2003
09/07/1975 DOD
california resident

Sandra Ortiz Taylor
4/27/36, USA

Title: Power; Politicos' Paradiso
2003

S. Ortiz Taylor

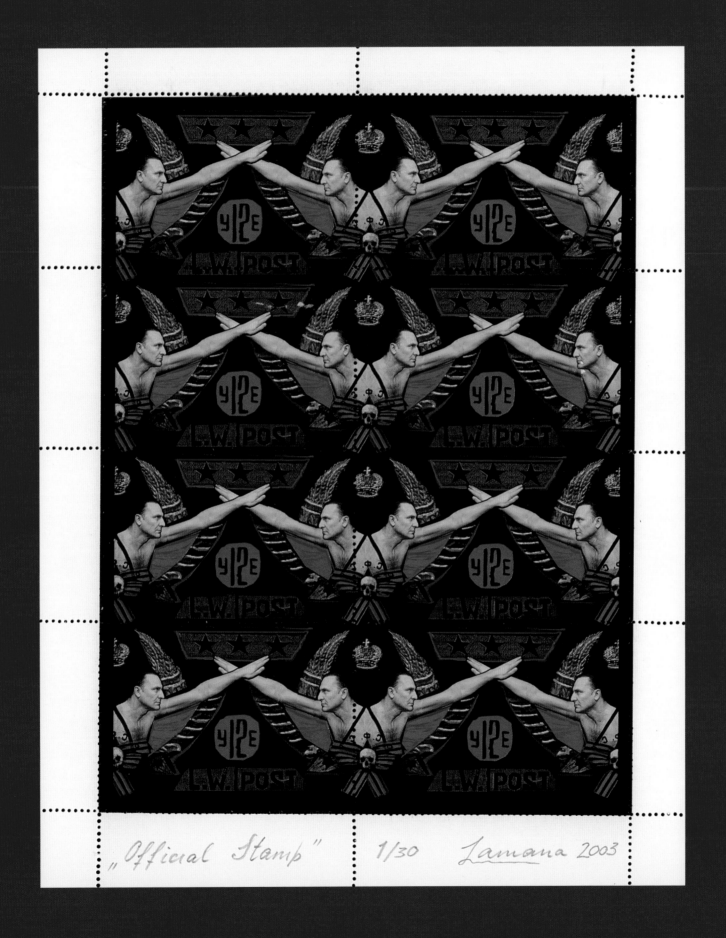

„Official Stamp"   1/30   Lamana 2003

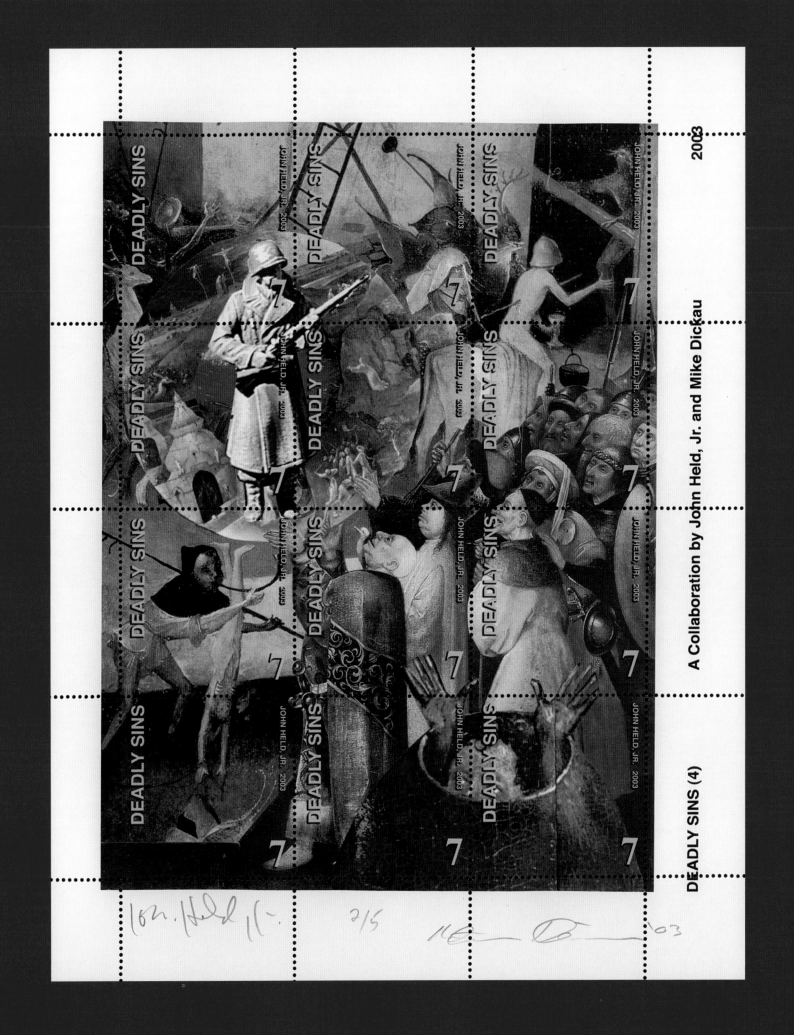

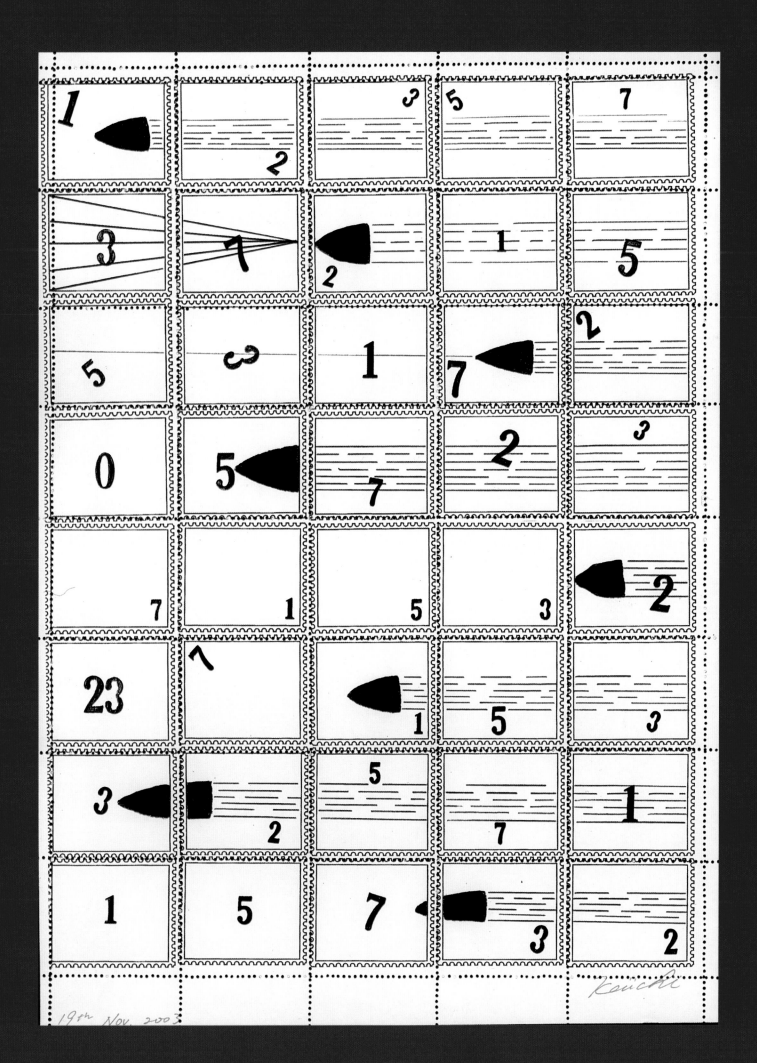

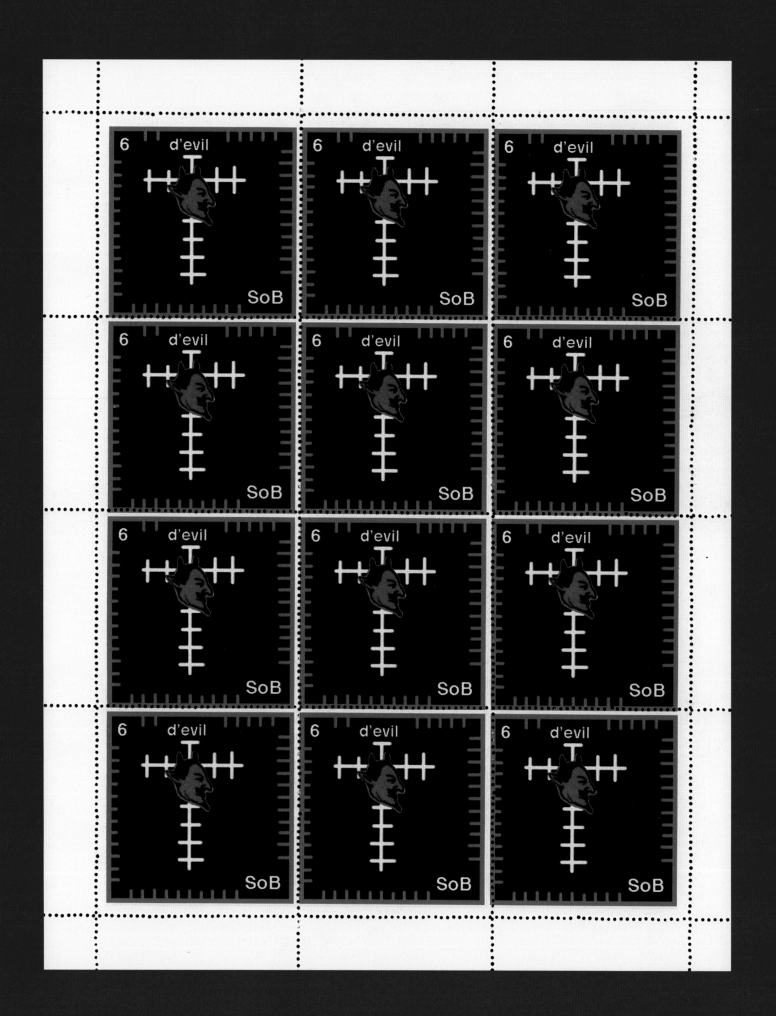

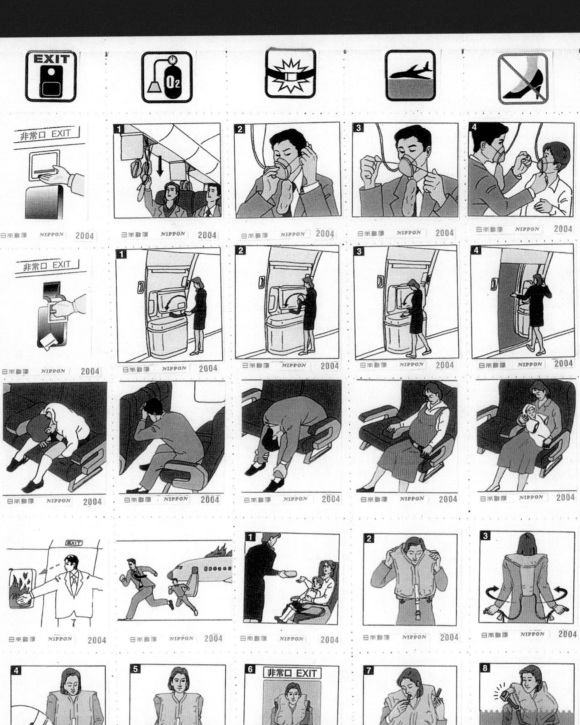

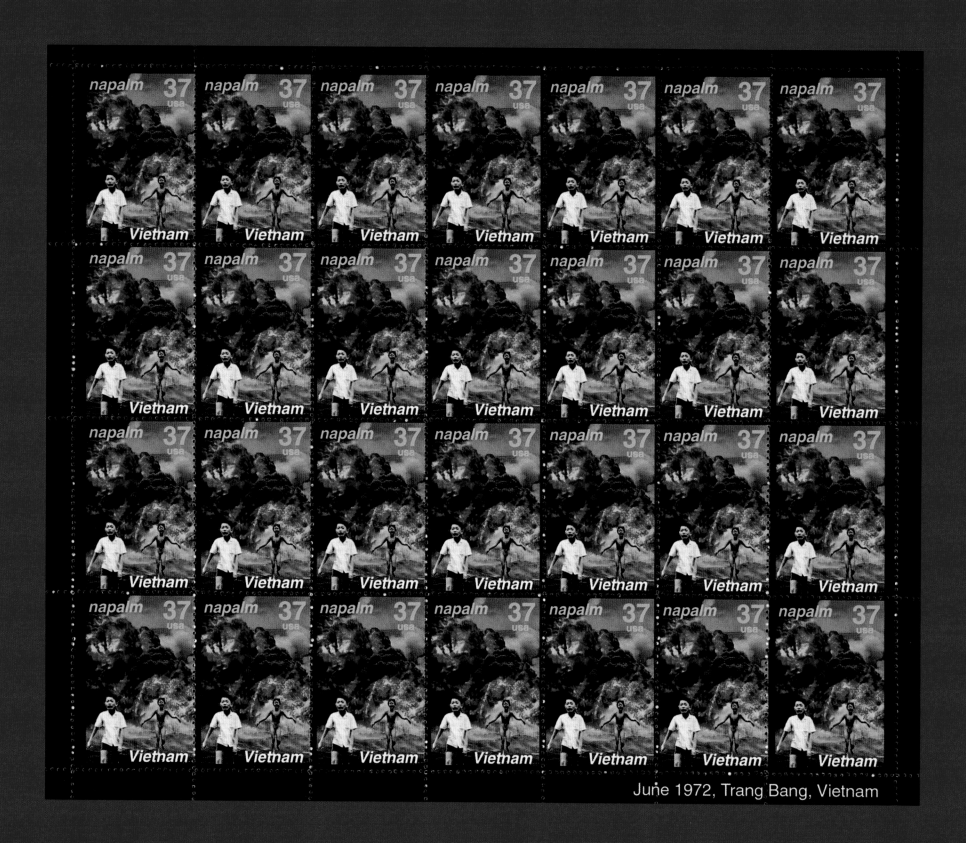

June 1972, Trang Bang, Vietnam

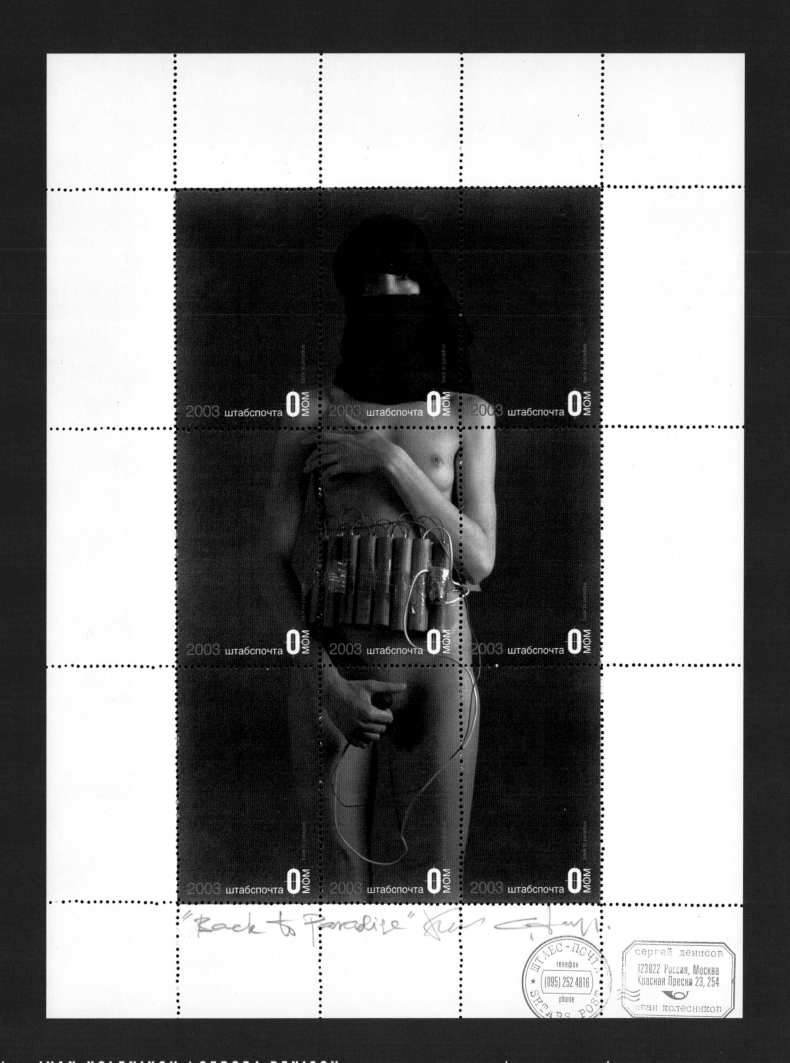

Who Pays

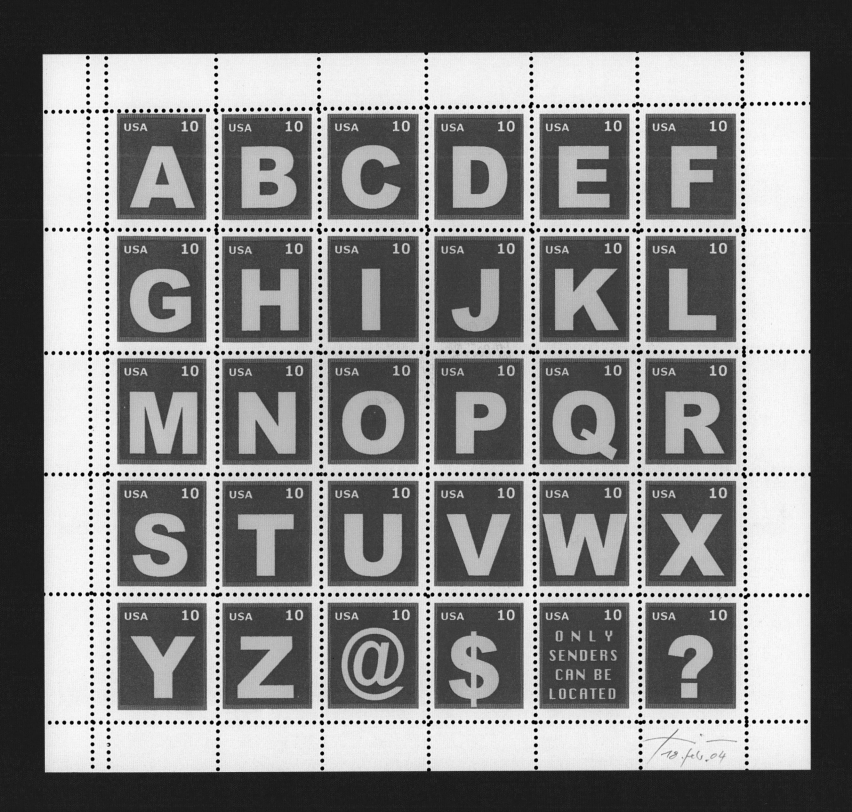

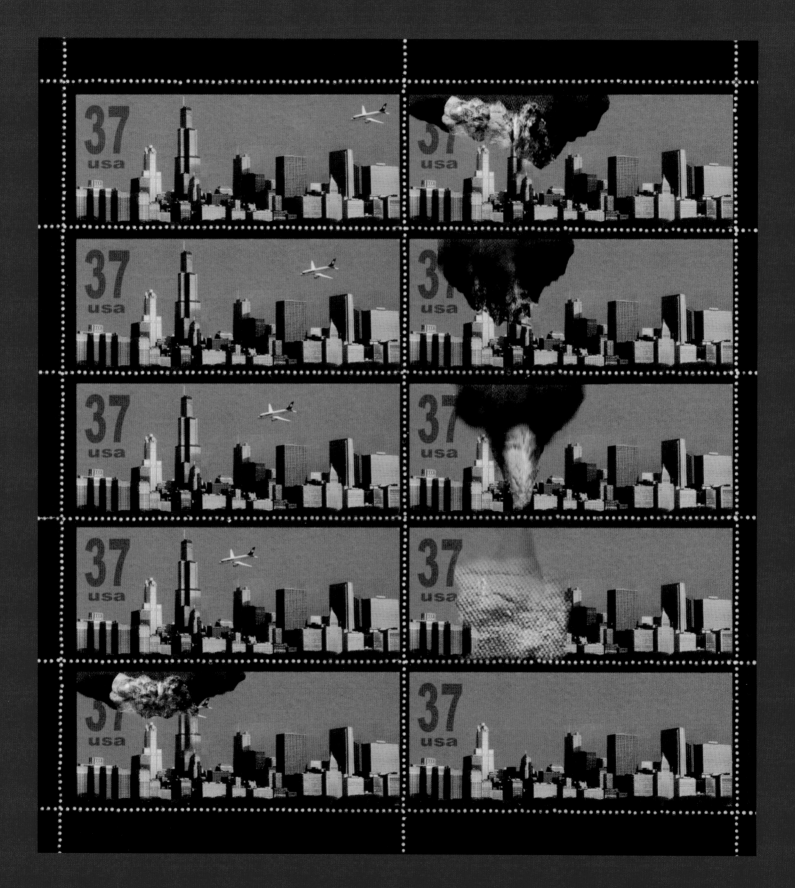

Study of Explosion

by TIMOTHY SHORTELL

Religion & Morality
A CONTRADICTION EXPLAINED

FRENCH SOCIOLOGIST EMILE DURKHEIM OBSERVED THAT RELIGION WAS THE ROOT OF science. Religion, he said, was the first human attempt to systematically explain the world. Durkheim thought that religious rationality would wither away in modern times (for him, the early twentieth century) because scientific rationality would replace it, by virtue of its superior explanatory power. Alas, he seems to have gotten this one wrong.

But Durkheim was right about the genealogy of thought. Modern religion is an elaboration of a belief in magic. In the absence of a scientific explanation of events and institutions, faith in magical powers, fetishization of nature, and overinterpretation of random variation are inevitable. Durkheim expected religion to fall out of fashion as the outright belief in magic had, for the same reason. For anyone with the least education, the superior power of scientific thinking is obvious. Only a willful ignorance could lead to any other conclusion.

This is where we find ourselves. We live in a world that wants the fruits

IT IS NO ACCIDENT THAT THE HISTORY OF WORLD RELIGIONS IS...

of scientific labor, but refuses the mental discipline of scientific rationality. Just like children, we want to have our cake and to eat it too.

Religions have persisted, despite their inability to explain the modern world. Here, in fact, we have a stunning reversal: religions play up the "essential mystery" of modern life. Since the world is too complex to understand all at once, in its entirety—even for the scientist—all of us will sometimes shake our heads in wonder at the turn of events in which we find ourselves. Many will find this uncertainty anxiety-provoking, and will look around for a convenient escape.

As social organizations, religions have a dramatic power that hides their essential irrationality. They persist today because they are so effective at constructing group identities and at setting up conflict between the in- and out-groups. For all religions, there is an "us" and a "them." All the ritual and the fellowship associated with religious practice is just a means of continually emphasizing group boundaries and hostility. It is no accident that the history of world religions is a history of violence, hatred, and intolerance. The in-group has exclusive access to the truth, so the out-group need not—indeed, should not—be listened to; they can only deceive. And, being liars, and thus, evil, they forfeit their rights as equal members of the community. This is the poisonous logic of religious irrationality.

All modern religions are ideological: they insist on a total, though contradictory, system of beliefs and evaluations. Complete acceptance is the only way to escape the uncertainly of modernity. For this reason, religion without fanaticism is impossible. Anyone whose mind is trapped inside such a mental prison will be susceptible to extreme forms of behavior. All religions foment their own kind of holy war.

The reader might point out that some believers are more bland and mild than fire and brimstone. Those whose devotion is moderate are, perhaps, only cowardly fanatics. They want the fellowship and the security but ignore the logic of the system to which they grudgingly adhere. They may be more numerous than the overt fanatics, but they will always have less influence. This is simply the operation of the rule of the lowest common denominator; in response to uncertainty, the exaggerated sense of confidence of the zealot will win over the crowd. If you doubt that this is true, consider modern politics. The same dynamic applies. This is why our political system has given birth to the "war on drugs" and "family values."

Faith is by definition not rational—that is, it is belief in the absence of verification. (If you do not think this is a fair definition of faith, look it up. I got this from the Merriam-Webster online dictionary, item 2b.) If every assertion were subject to question, the faithful would have to admit that they hold their beliefs without rational basis. If the public sphere were to promote the free contest of ideas, religious belief would wither under the scrutiny of scientific rationality, just as Durkheim expected. As with nationalism, faith is secured by appeals to emotion, not critical thinking. Emotion in crowds tends toward panic or violence. (Remember the rule of the lowest common denominator.)

In order to be protected from the harsh light of rational argument, the faithful want to make religion a taboo subject. Orthodoxy is supposed to be beyond question. Just as in totali-

A HISTORY OF VIOLENCE, HATRED AND INTOLERANCE

...RELIGIOUS TRADITIONS ARE BASICALLY ANTI-PLEASURE,

tarian states, where criticism of the government is a capital offense, the faithful would like to enforce an intellectual gag-order so that the barbarity of their regime goes unchallenged.

In every religious tradition, there is an orthodoxy with an elite (priests, ministers, rabbis, mullahs, etc.) to enforce it, and considerable effort is made to suppress dissent. Where religion is still powerful enough to influence politics—in places such as the U.S., Iran, Israel, for example—religious leaders seek to extend the reach of orthodoxy to the public sphere. We live at a time, alas, when more and more people are demanding that unpopular ideas be suppressed. Speaking freely is now an invitation to serious trouble.

It is no wonder, then, that those who are religious are incapable of moral action, just as children are. To be moral requires that one accept full responsibility for oneself. In order to act in the world as an adult, one must be able to recognize that the world is structured and the situatedness of all individual action. The choices that present themselves in the course of day-to-day living are influenced by social forces over which we have no control. Moreover, there is an element of randomness in the flow of events that prevents any of us from being able to predict fully what will happen next. Morality is a basis for making choices, in the context of a probabilistic world, embedded in a particular political economy.

Faith, like superstition, prevents moral action. Those who fail to understand how the world works—who, in place of an understanding of the interaction between self and milieu, see only the saved and the damned, demons and angels, miracles and curses—will be incapable of informed choice. They will be

unable to take responsibility for their actions because they lack intellectual and emotional maturity.

This is why Friedrich Nietzsche hated religion so much. Nietzsche despised weakness. He did not think of weakness primarily in terms of physical strength. Rather, he was referring to quality of character. In this regard, it is hard to imagine that anyone could disagree. Who would argue in favor of the virtue of bad character?

Well, we know who: priests, cops, and psychiatrists. We must be weak in order to be controlled. Like it or not, religion is one of the most effective institutions of social control. Though organized religions are sometimes at odds with governments, in a larger sense, the faithful are merely foot soldiers of the Spectacle. (This is Guy Debord's term to describe the form of modern consumer capitalism. It is an apparatus that encompasses capital and all superstructural institutions, such as religion and the media. In the Spectacle, we exist only as consumers. We are marketed products—consumables or ideas—based on our identities; to the Spectacle, we are nothing more than demographic targets.)

As foot soldiers, their job is to instigate widespread fear. This is why they see sin everywhere. Sin will bring punishment. An angry god is an effective rhetorical tool. Why fear? Because fear prevents us from being open to the varieties of beauty and pleasure around us. When we are afraid, we seek comfort in warm, enclosed spaces—literally and figuratively. The fearmongers hope to send us scurrying toward the safety of their prison. The strategy works, too. We can now understand why so many people turn to religion or shopping as a refuge from complexity.

WHICH IS WHY RELIGIOUS LAW IS SO OBSESSED WITH SEXUALITY.

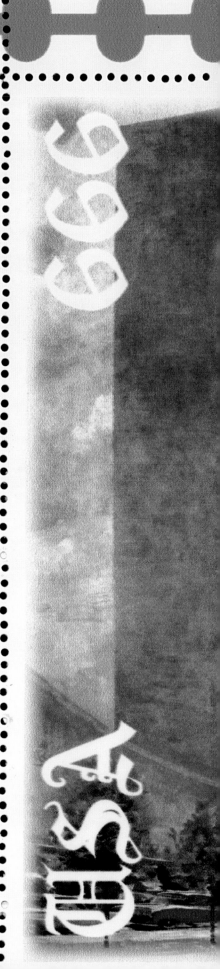

NGS TO DADDYS

MY HEART BELONGS TO DADDYS

MY HEART BELONGS TO

USA

2

USA

2

NGS TO DADDYS

MY HEART BELONGS TO DADDYS

MY HEART BELONGS TO

SOMEWHERE THERE IS A YOUNG FANATIC WHO...

Both function, albeit by different rituals and with different ideologies, to create the illusion of security. Like shoppers, believers are protected from the ugly truths of the real world.

The cost, of course, is the opportunity to explore what the world has to offer. Children must do what they are told. So, too, the faithful. At least children know that the power exercised over them keeps them from enjoying themselves. Those who surrender responsibility for their own moral action lack even that insight; to them, slavery is freedom.

Oh, dear reader, I know the argument: choosing to be servile is not the same as being forced to be servile, therefore, religious faith really is liberating. This is utter nonsense. Rationalists see this example of mental gymnastics for what it is, self-delusion.

In contrast to the believer is the artist. (I am referring here, of course, to ideal types, in the manner of the great German social scientist, Max Weber.) The artist is an exemplar of courage. Creativity requires a boldness and fortitude that can be fruitfully applied to everyday living. The artist must have a scientific rationality—in the sense of using experimentation to discover—otherwise, his work will be insipid or trite. This rationality brings one, also, to a new manner of living in the moment. It engenders a skepticism that reduces the shrill hysteria of these henchmen of the Spectacle to background hiss. Thus, one can concentrate on the humanizing qualities of beauty and pleasure. In this way, true morality is possible.

The artist as an ideal type has two meanings, and it is important to distinguish between them. The first refers to a kind of person who produces art—that is, paints a painting, writes a poem, composes a musical piece, and so forth. This is the artist as a technician, someone who is skilled in *technê*, or craft of artistic design. When I refer to the artist, this is **not** the meaning I have in mind.

Rather, I am thinking of the second sense of the type. The artist is an aesthete. Whereas *technê* is a set of skills that may be acquired through practice, aesthetic awareness must be cultivated by a difficult discipline. It requires a certain habit of mind that is quite different from ordinary awareness. It is a sensitivity to the subtleties of beauty and sensual pleasure. It is a familiarity with the positive and negative aspects of stimulation, and an appreciation of the necessity of both forms. Whereas the artist as craftsman might produce a religious object of devotion, the artist as aesthete is diametrically opposed to the believer.

The artist as aesthete is fundamentally open to the full range of experiences of humanity. All religious traditions are basically anti-pleasure, which is why religious law is so obsessed with sexuality. You can't be fully human if you are unrelentingly hostile to pleasure. The aesthete is defined by openness to the sensual world just as the believer is defined by a closedness to it. Lacking the proper appreciation for humanity, believers can be motivated to commit unspeakable acts. (A mob of believers is common enough in contemporary society; we see such mobs in the news regularly. A mob of aesthetes is impossible.) This closedness to pleasure is a necessary condition for the kind of suffering that makes a young person susceptible to irrational persuasion. Those who, at their core, resent beauty and pleasure will be only too willing to engage in hatred and violence.

On a personal level, religiosity is merely annoying—like pop music or reality television. This immaturity represents a signifi-

THINKS KILLING YOU WILL BE HIS TICKET TO HEAVEN.

THE AESTHETE IS DEFINED BY OPENNESS TO THE SENSUAL WORLD...

cant social problem, however, because religious adherents fail to recognize their limitations. So, in the name of their faith, these moral retards are running around pointing fingers and doing real harm to others. One only has to read the newspaper to see the results of their handiwork. They discriminate, exclude, and belittle. They make a virtue of closed-mindedness and virulent ignorance. They are an ugly, violent lot.

Here again, the temperate reader might sound a note of caution. "They are not all like that," he might say. No, they are not all like that. But that is not the point. Not all racists engage in lynching, either. It only takes a few. Soon enough, you have a mob and someone ends up dead. (Remember the rule of the lowest common denominator.)

Christians, in particular, like to think that religious violence is a problem restricted to other faiths. This is, in part, because the bloodiest days of Christianity, it would seem, are in the past. Most believers conveniently forget just how much blood is on their hands, historically speaking. Don't be fooled by such amnesia. In the heart of every Christian is a tiny voice preaching self-righteousness, paranoia, and hatred; the voice is louder inside the heads of the fundamentalists, of course, but it is there in the others' heads too. For theirs is a vengeful god. Those who believe that they are acting out "the divine plan" are the most dangerous sort in the contemporary world. Make no mistake.

It is curious, isn't it, how many believers are ignorant of the history of their own religion? Most know only the stories told in their scriptures, as if that substituted for genuine history. Some may even attempt to be balanced by acknowledging vague acts of wrongdoing in the distant past—so vague and distant as to be disconnected from the present. (I am reminded of George Carlin, playing the role of the Cardinal in *Dogma*: "Mistakes were made." Always use the passive voice to avoid responsibility!) This sloppy recollection is a clear sign that critical thinking has been banished. As a result, the blood is still flowing. Christians attack gays and lesbians because "homosexuality is a sin." Christians kill health care providers because "abortion is a sin." Lots of forms of lesser violence, too, such as child molestation. And so on.

Can there be any doubt that humanity would be better off without religion? Everyone who appreciates the good, the true, and the beautiful has a duty to challenge this social poison at every opportunity. It is not enough to be irreligious; we must use our critique to expose religion for what it is: sanctimonious nonsense.

This is not a duty that we should take lightly. It will be increasingly dangerous in a society defined by fear. Those who call our attention to inconvenient facts, as we do, will be subject to special opprobrium. There will be hate-filled letters. (I've received my share.) There will be violence, too. Somewhere there is a young fanatic who thinks killing you will be his ticket to heaven.

We must not shrink from the task. It won't be easy; shifting the momentum of history never is. In a sense, ours is a fool's errand, but it is not folly. We may not actually hasten the demise of religion—that would be too much to hope for—but we can slow down the slide to the bottom. Within the Spectacle, there are only momentary spaces of freedom. This is what we fight for. Our work exposing the contradiction between religion and morality will, perhaps, preserve temporarily the freedom to think.

JUST AS THE BELIEVER IS DEFINED BY CLOSEDNESS TO IT.

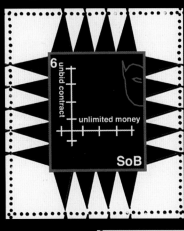

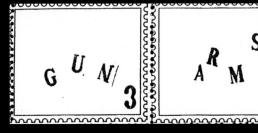

"What we observe is not nature itself but nature exposed to our method of questioning."

— WERNER HEISENBERG

131

(ABR)AXIS of LIVE/EVIL   (ABR)AXIS of LIVE/EVIL

$(^{1}/_{2}+^{1}/_{2})^{n}$ $(^{1}/_{2}+^{1}/_{2})^{n}$

PALINDROME REPUBLIC   PALINDROME REPUBLIC

134

'04 GREED

DOMINANCE 04

6   6   6

133

121

And now, I declare that you $

DIALOG 04 USA

MICHAEL HERNANDEZ DE

How can you get so upset, because I love the envelope you send. - Is it perhaps you didn't understand what I wrote you ???

U K   3

A R M S   3

G U N   3

129

AGGRESSION

Gogolyák post 2004

123

pwb post

pwb post

136

135

DEADLY SINS   DEADLY SINS

JOHN HELD, JR. 2003   JOHN HELD, JR. 2003

7   7

nika Helbing
er-Meinhof Post

Elke Callsen
Baader-Meinhof Post

125

ASSETS

127

37 USA   ASS POST

РОДИНА - ИГОРЬ ИОГАНСОН - ОТЕЧЕСТВО РОДИНА - ИГОРЬ ИОГАНСОН - ОТЕЧЕСТВО РОДИНА - ИГОРЬ ИОГАНСОН - ОТЕЧЕСТВО

ЦЕНА 4 КОП

ЦЕНА 3 КОП

ЦЕНА 5 КОП

МАТЬ

МАТЬ

ТВОЯ

POST OF NEW RUSSIA   POST OF NEW RUSSIA   POST OF NEW RUSSIA

7/50

02

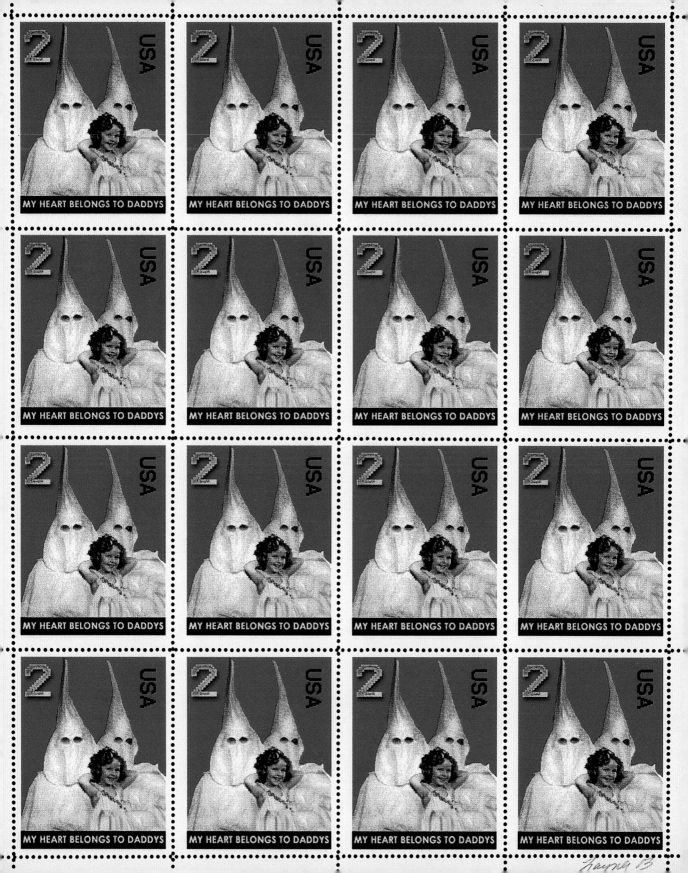

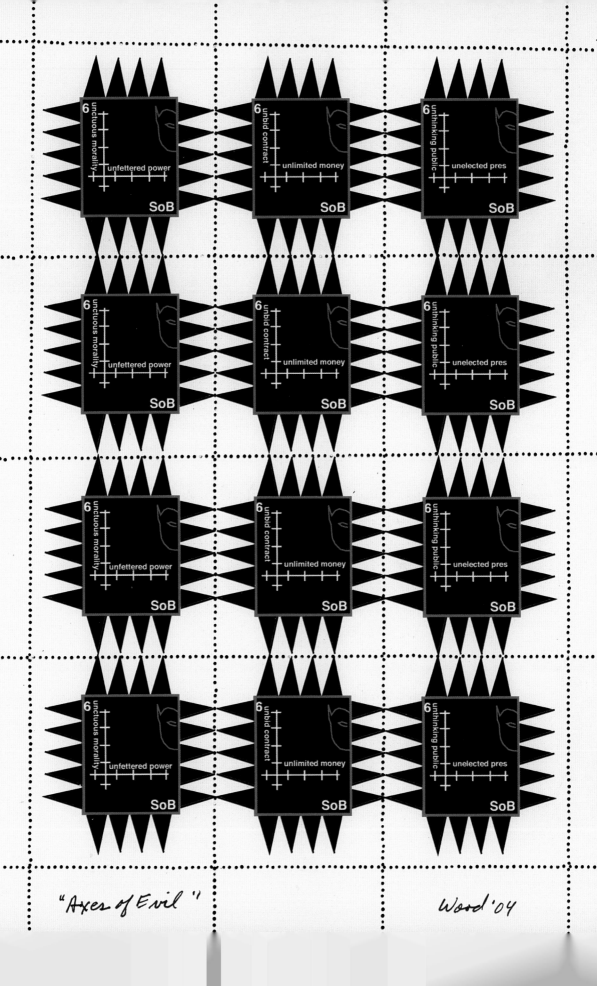

"Axes of Evil"

Wood '04

a letter to H.R.Fricker

And now, I declare that you stop making baby art and start making the real thing.   MHdL

DIALOG 04 USA

MICHAEL HERNANDEZ DE LUNA
How can you get so upset, because I love the envelope you send. - Is it perhaps you didn't understand what I wrote you ???

DIALOG 04 USA

MICHAEL HERNANDEZ DE LUNA
I think perhaps you might be a bit egocentric HR in your ATTITUDE as a MAIL ARTIST.
Is this true?

DIALOG 04 USA

MICHAEL HERNANDEZ DE LUNA
Why do all you Europeons get so upset and insulted at the drop of a penny?

DIALOG 04 USA

MICHAEL HERNANDEZ DE LUNA
I don't understand your anger for being an educated person / artist. Like your work there just words and sentences...
And my words I believe were very kind to you.

DIALOG 04 USA

MICHAEL HERNANDEZ DE LUNA
I am rewriting the Jeju Accord, because the ideas that I signed on are a pile of shit !!!
Like your attitudes !!!

DIALOG 04 USA

MICHAEL HERNANDEZ DE LUNA
Wake UP Man
MAIL ART is dead, along with DADA, along with your peanut FLUX-ASS attitudes.

DIALOG 04 USA

MICHAEL HERNANDEZ DE LUNA
I declare your FUCK'n world is over Ray Johnson told me telepathically from his other world !!!!!

DIALOG 04 USA

MICHAEL HERNANDEZ DE LUNA
ARE all you MAIL ARTIST,all so baby; like a balloon filled egos ????????????

DIALOG 04 USA

MICHAEL HERNANDEZ DE LUNA
Stop pretending to be over inflated ego maniacs and artists that cry like whining animals

DIALOG 04 USA

AM I being too hard, per-haps even unnecessary, however you stupid idiot

DIALOG 04 USA

MICHAEL HERNANDEZ DE LUNA
you must be a young man to behave in such a way. Are you in any way related to Padin ?

AXIS of EVIL 04 USA

MICHAEL HERNANDEZ DE LUNA
PROTEST ALL MAILART Cry-inns; Today!!!!!!
Stop cryiung about the past dead-history and events and join the 21 Century.

MAIL ARTIST, you can go to sleep now, and cry under your blankets of ego & worthlessness, and bad anti-art / establishment / and whatever. MHdL

from Michael Hernandez de Luna

H.R. Fricker 12. Februar 2004
© USA - United Suspected Artists

aggressive correspondence school of art / 1986

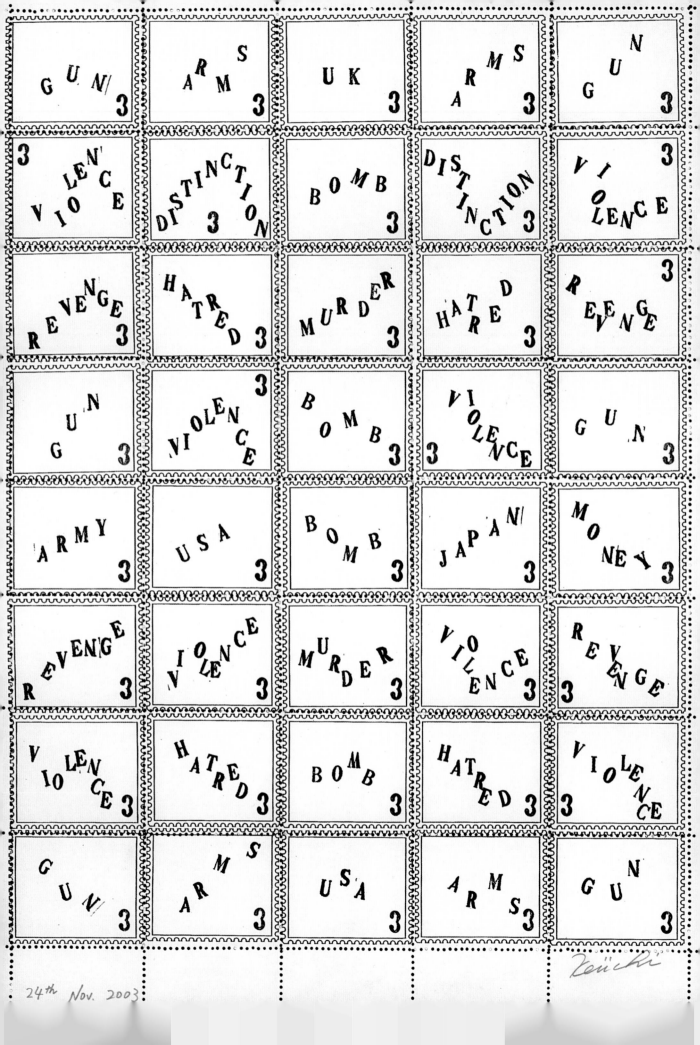

POST·NEO

PLAYING GOD
WITH NATURE

The American Sphincter   ASS POST

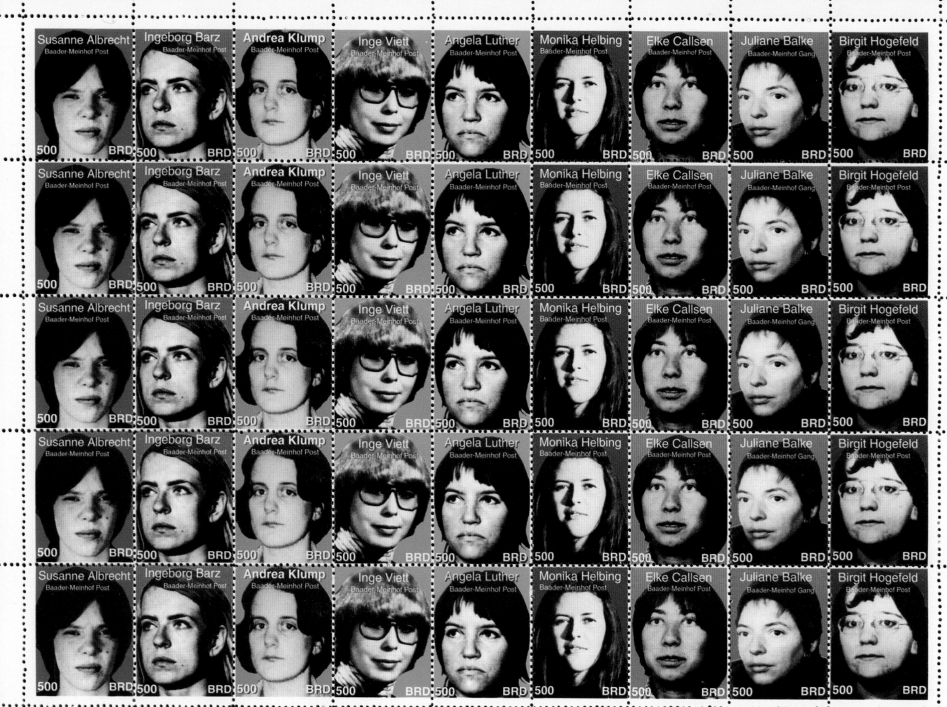

The Baader-Meinhof Girls

MEXICO ILUSIÓN 9

CHILE VIOLENCIA 9

URUGUAY VERGÜENZA 9

MEXICO ILUSIÓN 9

CHILE VIOLENCIA 9

URUGUAY VERGÜENZA 9

old stuff from 1998

(ABR)AXIS of LIVE/EVIL

$(1/2+1/2)^n$

PALINDROME REPUBLIC

(ABR)AXIS of LIVE/EVIL

$(1/2+1/2)^n$

PALINDROME REPUBLIC

(ABR)AXIS of LIVE/EVIL

$(1/2+1/2)^n$

PALINDROME REPUBLIC

(ABR)AXIS of LIVE/EVIL

$(1/2+1/2)^n$

PALINDROME REPUBLIC

DOGFISH

© Robert C. Rubin
2004

kill them all 0¢

DEATH FROM BELOW

0¢ all them kill

Give Us Liberty

USA

Or Give Us Death

Peace by

Super!or Firer Power

let god figure it out

DEATH FROM ABOVE

tuo ti erugif dog tel

Liberty thur Death

Allan Pocius

Mr. Lotto

AXIS OF EVIL by ANNA BANANA, FEBRUARY 2004

pwb post

pwb post

pwb post

pwb post

pwb post

pwb post

pwb post

pwb post

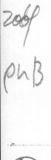

pwb post

pwb post

pwb post

pwb post

pwb post

pwb post

pwb post

pwb post

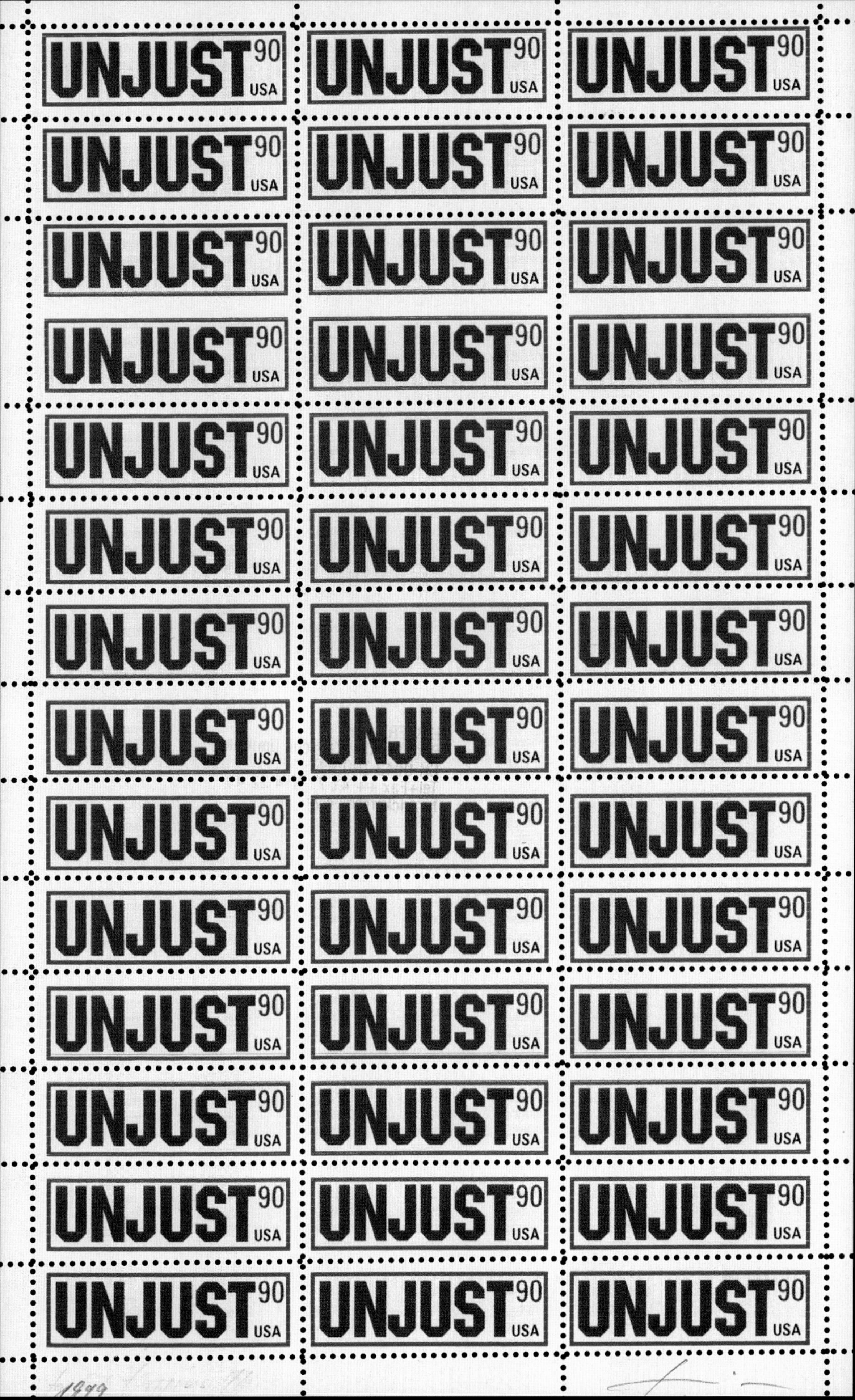

PRAXIS OF EVIL: HOW TO JUSTIFY ANYTHING

FOR THOSE WHO WISH TO INDULGE, JUSTIFY AND PROPAGATE EVIL
THERE ARE THREE RULES OF THUMB:

by **DAVID BADE**

MOST OF THE PEOPLE IN ANY POSITION TO CENSOR or otherwise respond to whatever the artist might wish to get away with have no more of an idea of what "Art" is than the professors of art, but are cowed and awed by the very words "Art" and "Artist" and have no desire to be considered uncultured, censorious Pollyannas.

So call it Art – whatever it really is does not matter – and you can get away with rape and murder.

If anyone is actually prudish enough to protest, you can count on the advocates of freedom of speech and artistic license to rush to your defense even if they know nothing at all about you or your "Art."

IF "ART" DOESN'T WORK OUT AS WELL AS YOU

would like, or if you want to get a job teaching,

then call whatever you say or do "speaking truth to power" or some other variation on "freedom of speech," for this is indeed protected by the Constitution of the United States of America.

You have not only all the intellectuals but also the Supreme Court on your side. (The only problem that you could conceivably encounter is that if your case actually gets to the Supreme Court, one or more of those old buzzards may actually look at, read and consider what you have said or written, etc.)

IF NEITHER ART NOR INTELLECTUAL FREEDOM

nor Freedom of Speech shelters your crimes and evil intentions, then sneak it in as religion.

Better to attach yourself to an established religion and try to find some verse in the Bible or the Koran that you can twist to suit your purposes,

but if that does not work, then find some sect or cult; when all else fails, invent your own religion, for that is a time-honored tradition. As long as it is not too severe, persecution can only help your cause, just as it does in the case of art and of freedom of speech. Warning: the Religion approach works better with the Right than with the Left. Not only will doing this mean the loss of all the friends and money garnered under the previously mentioned approaches, but you may also have to share your bed with Jimmy Swaggart, so use Religion only as a last resort!

157

Ultimate Peace

0c WORLD POSTAGE

0c WORLD POSTAGE

154

DEICIDE 2|0 0|4

Gogolyák post

147

DEADLY SINS

DEADLY SINS

JOHN FIELD JR. 2003

7

7

161

ULL OF LIGHT

JOEL SMITH COMMEMORATIVE TON

159

E MVP L I L

152

6

E V L

SoB

148

37

We Love to Hate

UNITED STATES

160

AN AMERICAN STORY   *MIKE DICKAU*

I THINK I'LL GO DOWN TO BEN AND BOB'S WHISKEY BAR, DRINK MY FILL, AND SHOOT THE FIRST PERSON WHO PISSES ME OFF...

163

rausch post

JUNIO 1973   30 CTS.

AY!

uruguay

JUNIO 1973   4 c

uruguay

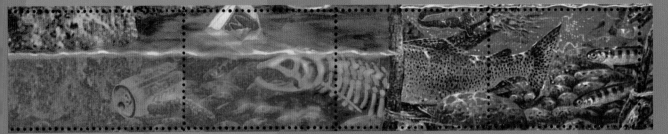

155

149

37

MY LORD! He's Pissn'

37 usa

MY GOD! He's Black!

156

T IF THINE EY

E BE EVIL THY

EL SMITH COMMEMORATIVE TONGUE

JOEL SMITH COMMEMORATIVE TONGUE

BoneDry

USA 69$

"There is no sin except stupidity." – OSCAR WILDE

150

pwb post

1998

162

pwb post

1998

pwb post

1998

pwb post

1998

pwb post

1998

cambodia 37 usa

Pol Pot 1970

cambodia 37 usa

Pol Pot 1970

153

37 usa

t for terrorist

146

UNIO

1973

30 CTS.

AY!

uruguay

151

MINSITRY OF TRUTH

REVENUE

$2

MINSITRY OF TRUTH

REVENUE

$3

158

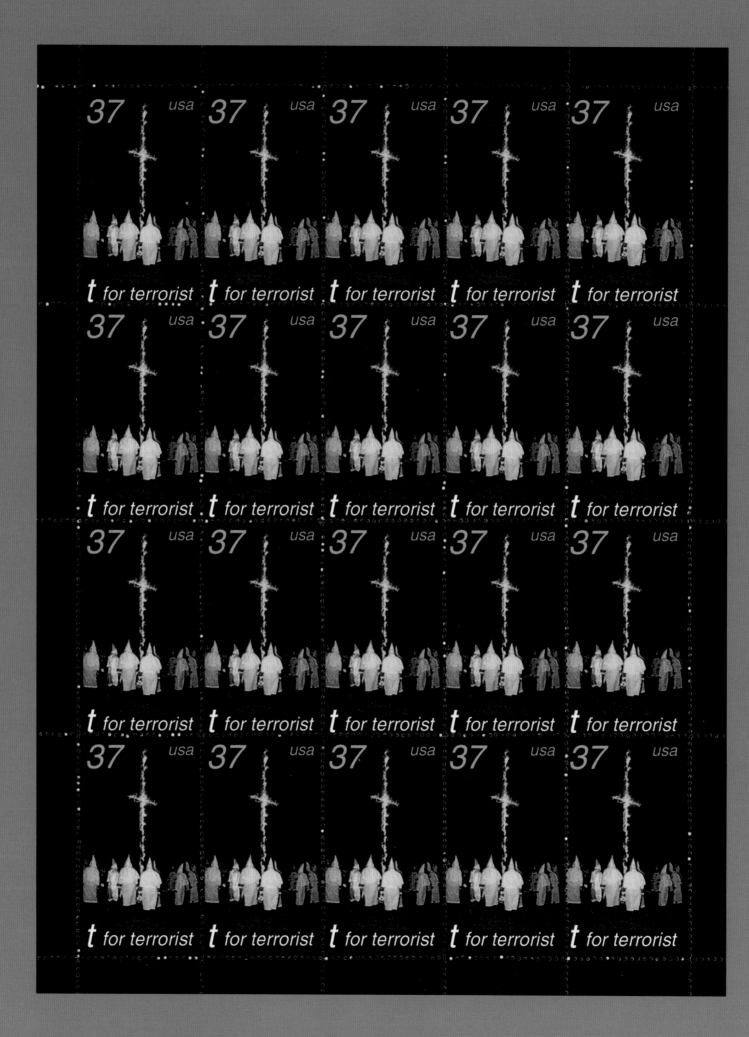

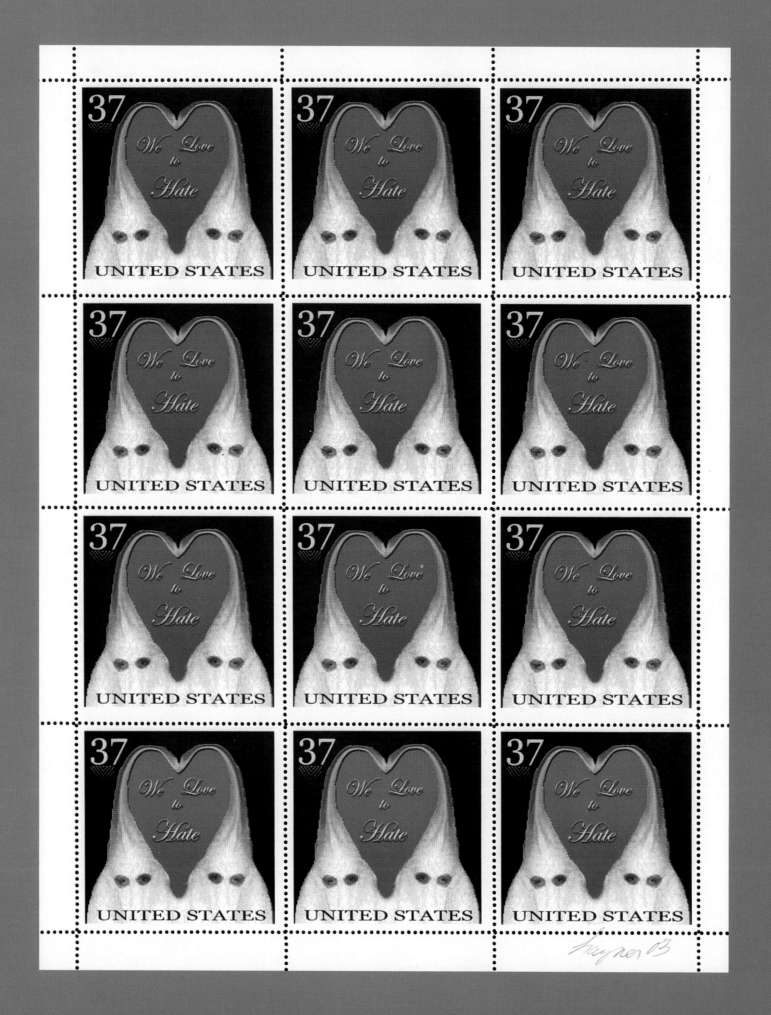

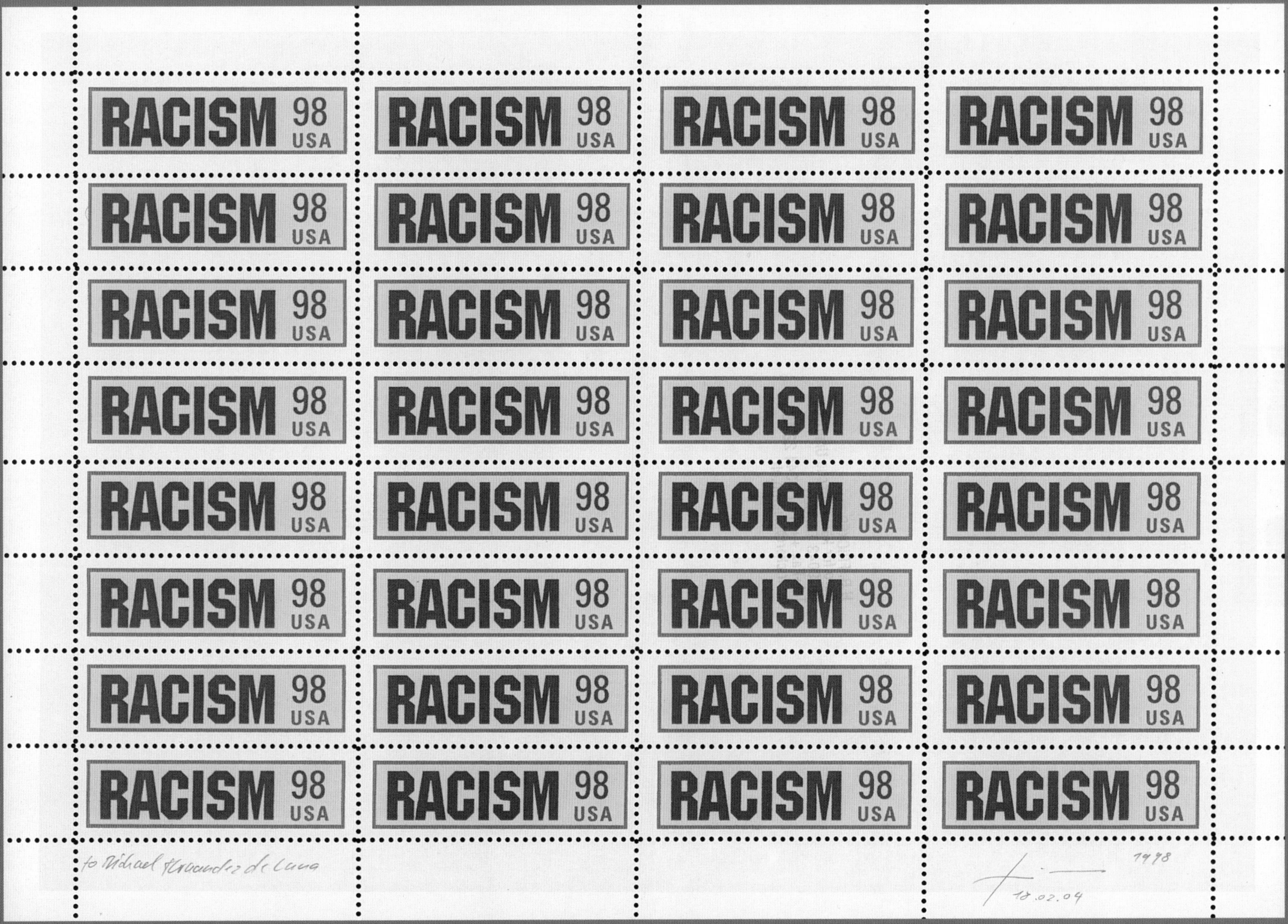

Slow Death

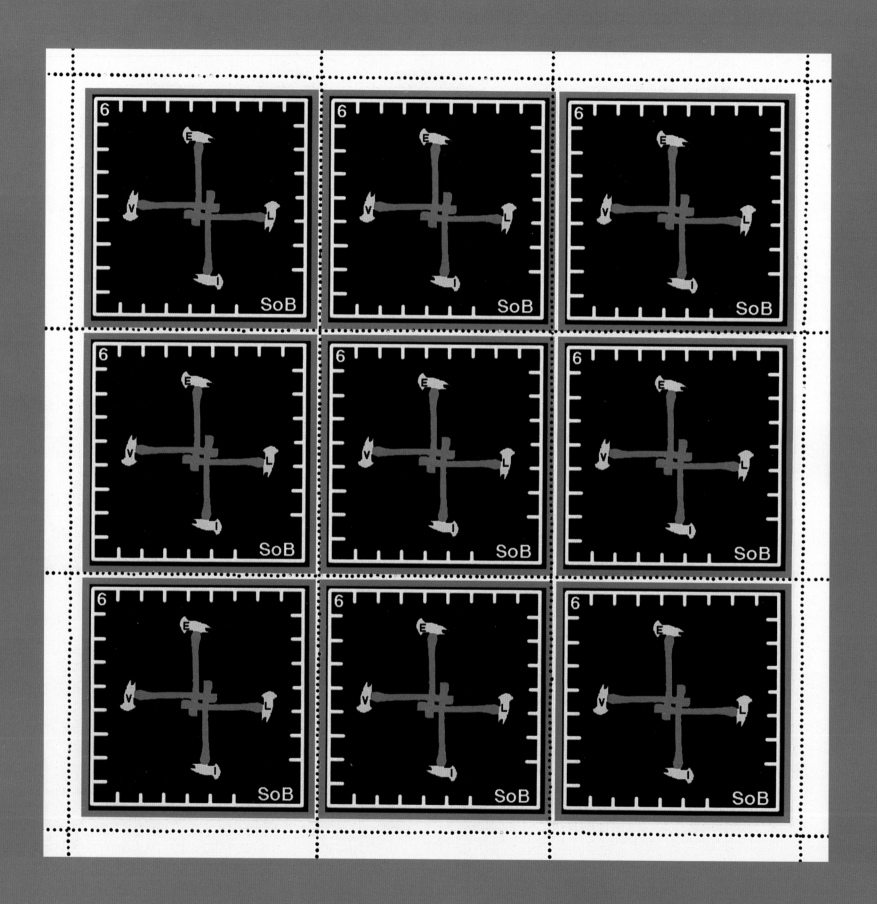

PACIFIC COAST RAIN FOREST

www.artgonepostal.com

© STEVE SMITH 2000

THE NATURE OF AMERICA

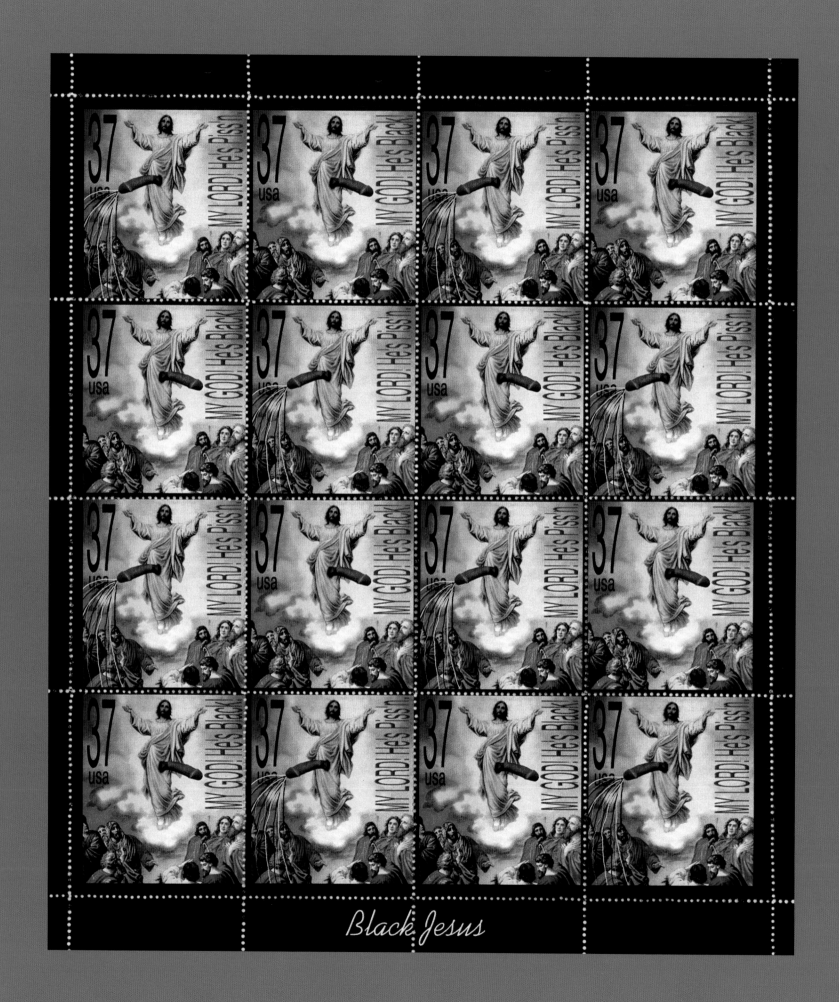

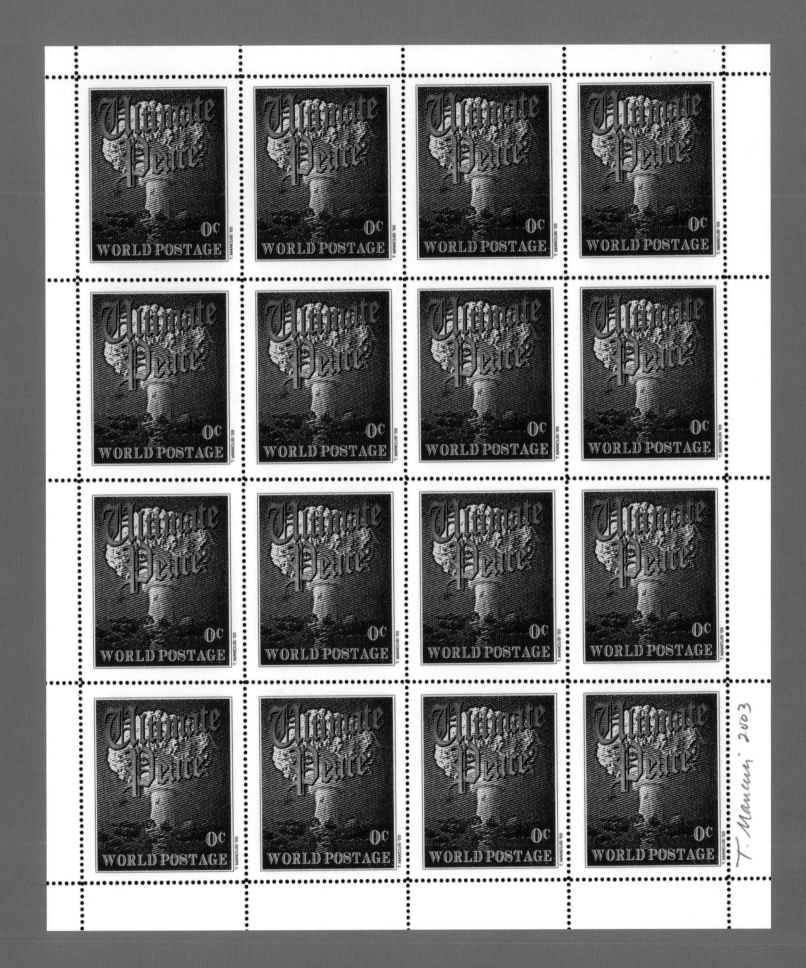

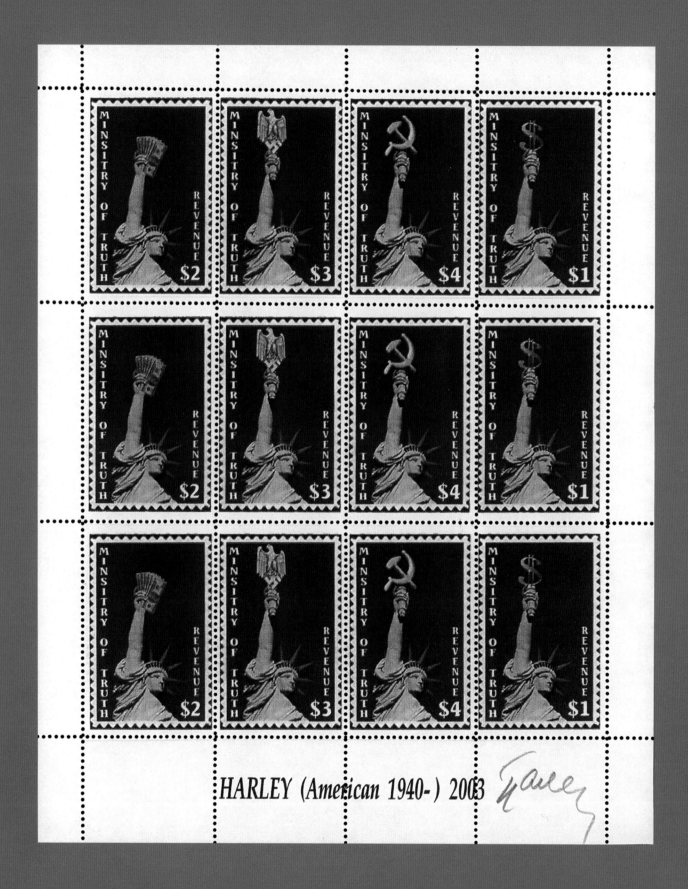

HARLEY (American 1940-) 2003

POST·NEO

Bicoastal cultural elite cheap, dark and plentiful

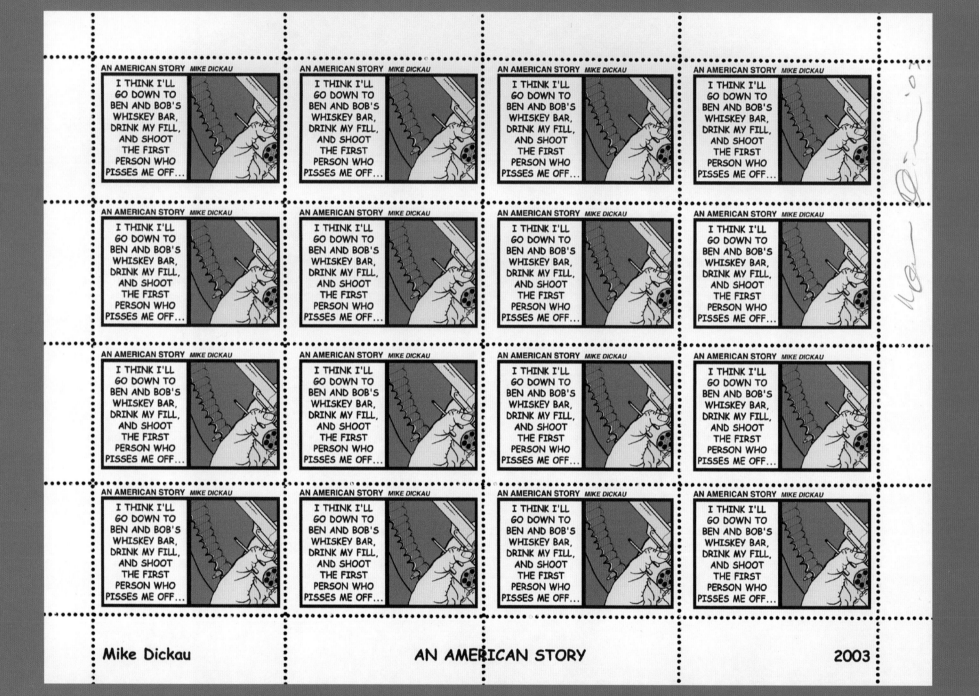

THE LIGHT OF

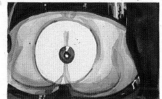

JOEL SMITH COMMEMORATIVE TONGUE

THE BODY IS T

JOEL SMITH COMMEMORATIVE TONGUE

HE EYE IF THER

JOEL SMITH COMMEMORATIVE TONGUE

EFORE THINE E

JOEL SMITH COMMEMORATIVE TONGUE

YE BE SINGLE

JOEL SMITH COMMEMORATIVE TONGUE

THY WHOLE BO

JOEL SMITH COMMEMORATIVE TONGUE

DY SHALL BE F

JOEL SMITH COMMEMORATIVE TONGUE

ULL OF LIGHT B

JOEL SMITH COMMEMORATIVE TONGUE

UT IF THINE EY

JOEL SMITH COMMEMORATIVE TONGUE

E BE EVIL THY

JOEL SMITH COMMEMORATIVE TONGUE

WHOLE BODY S

JOEL SMITH COMMEMORATIVE TONGUE

HALL BE FULL

JOEL SMITH COMMEMORATIVE TONGUE

OF DARKNESS

JOEL SMITH COMMEMORATIVE TONGUE

IF THEREFORE

JOEL SMITH COMMEMORATIVE TONGUE

THE LIGHT THA

JOEL SMITH COMMEMORATIVE TONGUE

T IS IN THEE BE

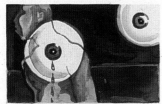

JOEL SMITH COMMEMORATIVE TONGUE

DARKNESS HO

JOEL SMITH COMMEMORATIVE TONGUE

W GREAT IS TH

JOEL SMITH COMMEMORATIVE TONGUE

AT DARKNESS

JOEL SMITH COMMEMORATIVE TONGUE

BUT IF THINE E

JOEL SMITH COMMEMORATIVE TONGUE

YE BE EVIL THE

JOEL SMITH COMMEMORATIVE TONGUE

JOEL Smith

WHOLE BODY S

JOEL SMITH COMMEMORATIVE TONGUE

HALL BE FULL

JOEL SMITH COMMEMORATIVE TONGUE

50/200

OF DARKNESS

JOEL SMITH COMMEMORATIVE TONGUE

IF THEREFORE

JOEL SMITH COMMEMORATIVE TONGUE

Mathew

by **JIM SWANSON**

PERFORATED

Man is what he believes – ANTON CHEKHOV

HITLER, BUSH, POL POT, ALBERT FISH, THE UNABOMBER/TRUMAN, HALLIBURTON, KKK, BABY BOMBERS, TERRORISTS, CATHOLIC PRIESTS, MOTHA' TERESA…ALL OF US SEE EVIL RESIDING IN THE WORLD AROUND US. BUT WHAT IS EVIL—DOES IT EVEN EXIST? WHAT DOES IT MEAN TO LABEL AN INDIVIDUAL OR A GROUP OF INDIVIDUALS OR BELIEFS AS EVIL?

The early Greek philosophers believed in essences, and evil was an essence. Plato saw us as fully formed in our essences at birth, while Aristotle believed that we learned our essences. The first Nature vs. Nurture debate.

The monotheistic religions saw life as a battle between the forces of good and evil, with the god granting man the power to choose the destiny for

EVIL

Demonization Has Consequences

USofA 37/100

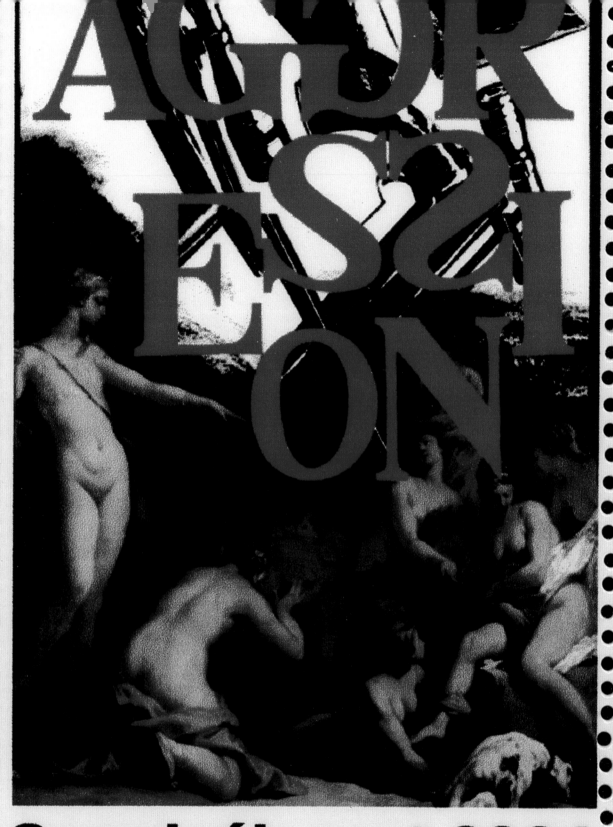
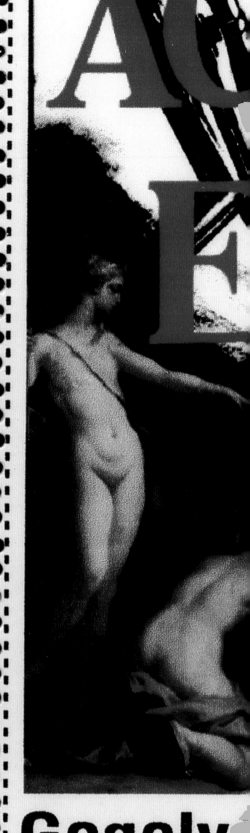

t 2004 **Gogolyák post 2004** **Gogoly**

mankind. The 3rd-century syncretic religion of the Manichaeans, which grew out of Christian, Gnostic, Zoroastrian, and Animistic religions, taught that there were two equally powerful deities—one good and the other evil. Always a dichotomy. Our animal minds have evolved to see the world in stark contrasts.

Christianity has waffled and most fundamentalist Christians and Muslims still use this doctrine of earthly conflict between light and dark, with the material world seen as dark. (Check out *Star Wars*, *The Matrix*, and many current movies for examples of Manichaean thought.)

In the 4th century, the North African St. Augustine, formerly an "evil" Pagan and Manichaean, became one of the leading Catholic scholars. Evil forces have been perceived by man forever, but Augustine tried to separate the evils which are not products of human agency—acts of nature—from those that come about through the agency or action of humankind—sinful acts. Augustine attacked the Manichaeans' belief in evil forces lying behind sinful acts because he saw it as a way of masking our own failings. Augustine, while obsessed with the sins of the flesh, did recognize that these beliefs granted too much simplicity and attendant denial.

> "Good and evil we know in the field of this world grow up
> together almost inseparably; and the knowledge of good is
> so involved and interwoven with the knowledge of evil, and
> in its so many cunning resemblances hardly to be discerned,
> that those confused seeds which were imposed upon Psyche
> as an incessant labor to cull out, and sort asunder, were not
> more intermixed." – **John Milton**, *Areopagitica*, 1644

A thousand years later Manichaean thought still survived and flourished as the resisters to the Reformation sought to survive in the New World. Our religious founders were being forced out of Europe because of their religious extremism and condemnation of their neighbors. There is an Australian bumper sticker, "Thank God we got the convicts and America got the Puritans," which succinctly summarizes our founding heritage. Protestant nationalism rode the Mayflower to Massachusetts in 1620. These beliefs evolved in a United States chosen by the "higher power" to defeat the forces of darkness—liberalism and scientific non-belief. Manichaean framing of life on this planet rode the forecastle and has always undergirded our belief systems. The main resistance to American Puritans came from reforming evangelism. Antinomians like Anne Hutchinson preached: "to the pure all things are pure." For the chosen all is permitted in the certainty of salvation. Antinomian beliefs fit well with the American myths of individualism and purpose—which have fueled many of our religious revivals. Since we have enshrined freedom of religion in our Constitution instead of creating a state religion we have found resistance always coming from within as opposed to growing out of non-religious beliefs. George W. Bush and Tony Blair see their inner religiosity as justifying whatever means they choose to employ. True Antinomians.

Moral Reconstruction: Christian Lobbyists and the Federal Legislation of Morality, 1865-1920. Gaines M. Foster (2002) observes: "A tradition of religion in politics based on faith in the law to make right, or at the very least, to create a moral order capable of making people behave morally, has always existed alongside the dominant voluntary and revivalist traditions."

Hellfire Nation: The Politics of Sin in American History. James A. Morone (2003) concludes: "When the established faiths—political, social, religious—begin to grow stale, there is always another hot American revival in the wings. Americans play many roles and believe many different things. But after more than three and a half centuries—for better and for worse—we remain Puritans all."

Jacob L. Talmon has proposed that in the 18th century two conflicting forms of democracy evolved: the traditionally recognized liberal democracy and concurrently a form called "totalitarian Messianic democracy." In American these two forms have always battled and are now "the most vital issue of our time." Because an organized secular belief system has never arisen in the United States the Messianic form has greater popular appeal, fueling our War on Evil.

Thought Contagion. Aaron Lynch (1996): "Proselytizing exposes Christians to many varied beliefs, and even to contrary proselytism. Therefore, Christians with memes that immunize them against contrary views stay Christian the longest. A belief that un-Christian messages are evil, even Satanical, is one such preservational meme. Christian hosts of this doctrine generally react with extreme distrust toward anyone expressing a contrary belief. That leads them to discard the contrary messages and remain Christian. This memetic immune mechanism thus confers preservational advantage to each faith that incorporates it, including Christianity.

"An 'evil apostasy' meme sometimes goes well beyond conferring memetic immunity, inspiring cases of religious aggression. ... Even if aggression against unbelievers only represses their free *expression*, it still limits the competitors' propagation."

All of the hierarchical primates need a defined social structure with rules and morals. As the largest brained primate, we have developed the most sophisticated ones. Since we have trouble understanding causation, place, and purpose, we assume a higher power and posit that higher power's intentions for us, thus creating theistic religions. Although many of us question beliefs in the gods, we still believe that His rules are essential for us to be moral. Many admitted atheists claim they are unable to trust a non-believing politician. We have become acculturated to the mythical existence of an ultimate source of direction. We do not question how the other primates survive, propagate, and evolve without knowing God's intentions. We have trouble accepting that we are one evolving and temporal life form among many. Thus, we resist the theory of evolution and the resultant cognitive dissonance and uncertainty. The simple truth is that there is no purpose, we are just specks on the windshield of time, and that evolution will continue with or without us.

Charles Darwin: "Our descent, then is the origin of our evil passions!! — The Devil under form of Baboon is our grandfather."

The Science of Good and Evil: Why People Cheat, Gossip, Care, Share, and Follow the Golden Rule. Michael Shermer (2004): "The myth of pure evil is the belief that evil exists separately from individuals, or that evil exists within people as something...driving them to perform evil acts....

"[A]s a noun...*there is no such thing as evil.* There is no supernatural force operating outside the realm of the known laws of nature and human behavior that we can call evil. Calling something or someone 'evil' gets us nowhere...does not lead us to a deeper understanding of the cause of evil behavior.

2002

2002

DAVID GILHOOLY, DEUS IRAE

DAVID GILHOOLY, DEUS IRAE

2002

DAVID GILHOOLY, DEUS

DAVID GILHOOLY, DEUS

"The real horror of Himmler is not that he was unusual or unique but that he was quite ordinary, and that he could have lived out his life as a chicken farmer, a good neighbor with perhaps somewhat antiquated ideas about people." [Quoted from "Holocaust historian and Himmler biographer Richard Breitman."]

"From an evolutionary perspective this makes sense. Individuals in our ancestral environment needed to be both cooperative and competitive, depending on the context and desired outcomes. …

"Evil forces do not exist, but evil acts are an all-too-human expression. Walt Kelly's cartoon character Pogo put it simply: 'We have met the enemy and he is us.' …

"Absolute morality generates absolute intolerance. And the problem is endemic to all absolute systems of thought, from religious to nonreligious, from libertarian to communist… ."

Claudia Koonz, in *The Nazi Conscience*, describes how they had a "powerful sense of right and wrong, based on civic values that exalted [their] moral righteousness." In a 1945 essay Hannah Arendt wrote, "The reality is that 'the Nazis are men like ourselves,' the nightmare is that they have shown, have proven beyond doubt what man is capable of." Samantha Power, writing on Arendt, proposes: "In order to move beyond superstition, which is what we cling to today, it is politics that has to be brought to bear. We are afraid, and fear is dangerous. It can justify excesses and can lead to escapism… and we can only hope, as Arendt did, that the tug toward apathy will be overcome by the lure of human improvement and self-preservation."

Tobias Wolff, in his novel *Old School*, writes: "had he learned nothing…he'd led his boys to consider the folly of obsession with purity—its roots sunk deep in pride, flowering in condemnation and violence against others and oneself. For years Arch had traced this vision of the evil done through intolerance of the flawed and ambiguous, but he had not taken the lesson to heart. He had given up the good in his life because a fault ran through it. He was not better than Aylmer, murdering his beautiful wife to rid her of her birthmark."

How we frame our views of the world limits and controls how we see the world. We expect Y to be crooked because of his skin color, his status, his heritage. We expect X to be on welfare because…"Poor women have babies to collect welfare," says the affluent, educated, middle-class, childless professional. A claim that can be easily shown incorrect, but it reinforces one's position and status. Degrees of status and available options are the greatest, inverse, determinants of childbearing. We don't know why we do or don't do something, but we are quick to create demons to defend our position in life. Those evil ones are why I haven't been sitting on the right hand of god in all MY glory. Perceiving evil in others is reflexive, an emotional response which has survival value for individual humans forced to make immediate decisions whether to fight or flee, but can destroy a culture or society.

All religions, from Christianity to Communism to Libertarianism and Fascism, are faith-based and animate oppression by perpetuating convenient myths and folk psychologies. All are conducting laboratory experiments on human life, but without the scientific principles of supervision, observation, and analysis. Using normative theories as opposed to analytical propositions. The unnatural masked as the natural.

Artistic visions are probably man's earliest attempts to create a scientific sensibility. Art stimulates an emotional response that predates language and stimulates brain activity. Art continues to provide insights into the non-conscious realms of human understanding, challenging science to understand. While art and the artist are inherently conservators—preserving and reifying the rapidly receding past—they also challenge the viewers' perceptions as well as exposing the artist's. Looking backward in order to understand and forward to anticipate the future, the artist and her creation confront us with their Janus faces. Why does an artist portray sexual priests? Homophobia and a belief that priests are more than human. Why does an artist portray Woody Allen as a "Kosher Pedophile"? Anti-Semitism and denial of the complexities of human sexuality. The images of suicide bombers hide the fact that suicide terrorists are no less sane or "rational" than we are. They are like us—all that is required is, in the words of Michael Bond, "a peculiar mix of social, cultural, and political conditions for a group to make the decision." As social animals we make group decisions. Robert Strange McNamara recalls, in Errol Morris' *The Fog of War*, that "rational" men brought the world to the brink of nuclear war three times in the '60s. "Rational" men can, and do, destroy life. McNamara admitted that he would have been tried as a war criminal for the fire-bombings of civilians if we had lost WWII.

We create an idealized, mythical narrative that cloaks the contingent nature of all life. Thus, creating monsters, discovering the other—in order to mask the mundane, pedestrian realities of embodied personal existence. Demonization—Michael Jackson (creative, but a black other), Catholic priests (whose turned head is homosexuality), Martha Stewart (who peddled dreams of purification and salvation, but was found normal), black men (supplying suburban whites with the drugs they crave because salvation is not available), crack moms (when we know that crack is not the cause of the intra-uterine growth retardation—poverty, malnutrition, and poor medical care are), scientists who search for the actualities of life (denying us our comfort blankets of folk myths).

The moderate skeptic, raised in religion lite, converts to Buddhism and thus grants credibility to the religious extremists by not refuting the myths of souls and eternal life. Like the fork-tongued Motha' Teresa who consigned the non-believers to suffering and damnation, the Buddhist convert glories in his own affluence while ignoring the suffering he is excusing. For Buddhists: SHIT HAPPENS. As long as the Buddhist converts are happy, the suffering have a chance for redemption in another life.

Islam, like all fundamentalist belief systems, always looks backward to received knowledge and purpose.

Man has fallen and must return to the state of grace. Bin Laden and Ashcroft crawled out of the same pestilent womb.

"…it was discouraging to hear the president describe Bin Laden as 'the evil one,' as if he were Satan himself, or a demon on Buffy the Vampire Slayer. We need to acknowledge that he's a murderous human being, however much we want to exclude him from the species.

"There's nothing supernatural about terrorism; human barbarism requires no help from the devil. People who believe that confronting terrorism requires God's help will disagree. But I suspect that what we mostly need now is self-control."–Wendy Kaminer.

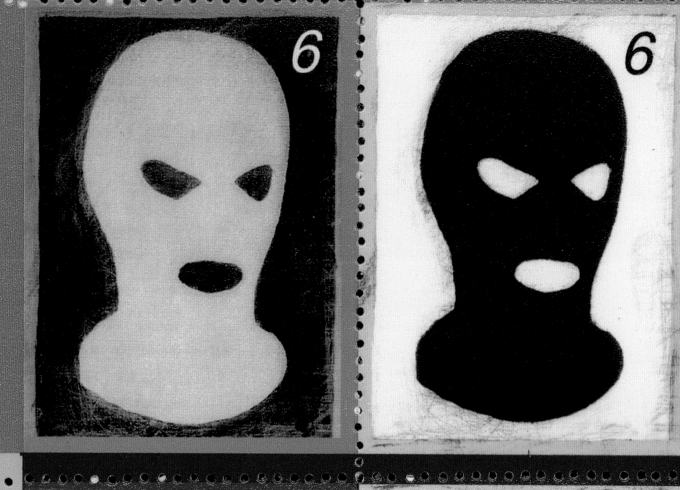

Denis Donogue recognizes "the delusion by which we think that reality coincides at every point with its appearances."

The White Queen Syndrome: screaming in agony before pricking her finger. We see suffering where it MAY occur and ignore where it IS occurring.

Life is a Confluence of Contingencies: Chaos, Coincidence, Chance, and Complexity.

Albert Einstein: "If the moon, in the act of completing its eternal way around the earth, were gifted with self-consciousness, it would feel thoroughly convinced that it was traveling its way of its own accord. …

"So would a Being, endowed with higher insight and more perfect intelligence, watching man and his doings, smile about man's illusion that he was acting according to his own free will."

Unlike the moon, we have the collective ability to hypothesize, test and verify how we act. Once we recognize that there is no purpose or necessity to our existence we can then understand the how of our existence. We are unable to personally understand our own individual existence, but we can ascertain that of man in general and of groups of humans in particular.

None of us are able to know personally why we do or do not have sex with another person and we do not individually understand our preferences and desires. This observation often elicits strong emotional responses, such as: "then you condone rape." There are two interesting aspects of this response.

One, the illusion of conscious, verbal free will which the responder believes controls sexual acts would also mediate the response—thus the responder would, if consistent, have asked what was meant by the observation. The responder, like all of us, is an emotional being subject to responding at a visceral level. Sexual attraction is a complex confluence of body states, pheromones, physicality, histocompatibility, opportunity, and more.

Two, there is a confusion of undesired sexual assault with consensual sexual congress which is followed by post-coital depression and/or regrets or confusion. Since we don't have conscious, verbal awareness of the processes of choice, we also don't understand why we have not attained the levels of happiness and enjoyment we have come to believe are essential for sexual encounters. We know that many species engage in serial and variant sexual acts, even those who engage in apparently monogamous long-term relationships, but in our confusion of essences we believe that we are materially different.

Philosopher Owen Flanagan, describing the work of neuroscientist Joseph LeDoux: "We know that a person can be conditioned—via their amygdala and thalamus—to be scared of things that really aren't worth being scared of. We also know that it is extremely hard to override what the amygdala 'thinks' and 'feels' simply by conscious rational thought."

Why We Hate. Rush W. Dozier, Jr. (2002): "The human limbic system poses a special danger because of its extensive connections to the neocortex, allowing us to fuse hatred and violence with the highest capacity of the human mind: meaning. Hate can override the fear of death in individual cases, but hate-oriented meaning systems can make such behavior systematic and widespread. Meaning is uniquely significant to human beings because, unlike virtually every other species, we are not born with specific instincts that tell us what to eat, where to live, how to organize our social groups, what tools to make, or whom to hate. The vast majority of our thoughts, emotions, and behaviors are shaped by meaning systems of our own creation… .

"Meaning rather than instinct is so overwhelmingly important to our species—and to our distinctive toolmaking cultures—that our limbic system has evolved a powerful tendency to blindly interpret any meaning system that we believe in as substantially enhancing our survival and reproduction…. Because of this unusual feature of the human brain, strongly held meaning systems are capable of decoupling our behavior from the objective criteria of survival and reproduction. If a particular group's strongly held meaning system calls on its members to be celibate and suicidal, their primitive brain areas will tend to presume that this is the best way to ensure their survival and reproduction, even though rationally, of course, it is not....

"The immense significance of meaning to human beings and its distinctive link in our species to the primitive emotional centers of the brain lay the groundwork for a primary source of hatred: fanaticism and intolerance.... Many of the most savage conflicts in history have involved quarrels over religious, political, and cultural systems of meaning....

"Without firm neocortical control, hate not only takes root, but also spreads. Specific, rational dislike can be transformed by the primitive neural system into obsessive hatred, and hate easily enlarges beyond its initial bounds because its core mechanism involves stereotyping and generalization.

Demonizing opponents can lead to limbic paranoia with absurdly generalized thinking, loose associations, and the rapid spreading of hatred among susceptible groups – a kind of hate contagion."

The Myth of the American Superhero. John Shelton Lawrence and Robert Jewett (2002): "[T]he following archetypal plot formula may be seen in thousands of popular-culture artifacts:

> A community in a harmonious paradise is threatened by evil; normal institutions fail to contend with this threat; a selfless superhero emerges to renounce temptations and carry out the redemptive task; aided by fate, his decisive victory restores the community to its paradisiacal condition; the superhero then recedes into obscurity.

"...It secularizes the Judaeo-Christian dramas of community redemption that have arisen on American soil, combining elements of the selfless servant who impassively gives his life for others and the zealous crusader who destroys evil. The supersaviors in pop culture function as replacements for the Christ figure... [reflecting] divine, redemptive powers that science has never eradicated from the popular mind [e.g., Neo in *The Matrix*].

"While the simplicity of myth and the prospect of vengeance offer special comforts in a time of mass murder, the notion of destroying evil on a worldwide basis may draw us toward spiraling conflicts that we can never hope to control.

"Only in a culture preoccupied for centuries with the question of salvation is the appearance

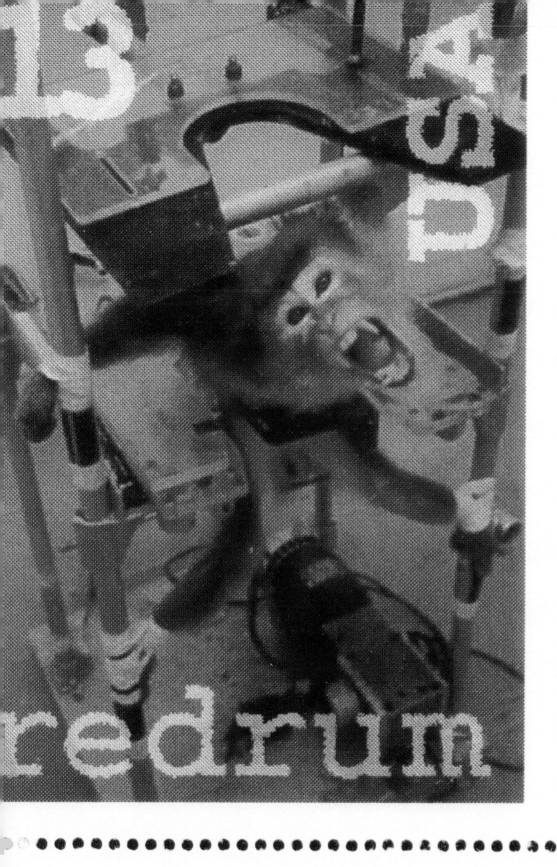

WE GROW THESE IN TEXAS

AGAINST THE DEATH PENALTY
PINE VALLEY COSMONAUTS, IL.

of redemption through superheroes comprehensible.

"The democratic institutions in monomythic stories are invariably pictured as incapable of coping with evil."

The Patriot Act subverts democracy to save our souls.

George W. Bush: "It is important for you boys and girls to know that we're fighting evil with good."

The President of Good & Evil: The Ethics of George W. Bush. Peter Singer (2004):

"[In order to] understand the context in which Bush [talks of evil], we need to remember that tens of millions of Americans hold an apocalyptic view of the world. According to a poll taken by *Time*, 53 percent of adult Americans "expect the imminent return of Jesus Christ, accompanied by the fulfillment of biblical prophecies concerning the cataclysmic destruction of all that is wicked."…Projecting this prophecy onto the world in which they live, many American Christians see their own nation as carrying out a divine mission. The nation's enemies therefore are demonized [thus, Axis of Evil]. …

"We all draw on our intuitions to decide what is right and what is wrong. In the hustle of everyday life it would be impractical to go back to first principles every time we need to make rapid moral decisions, or to pass judgment on what someone else has done. So we rely on a general intuitive sense that works most of the time."["Most of the time" does not protect us from those times it does not work.]

Leni Riefenstahl's classic 1934 documentary propaganda for the Hitler's Reich is very aptly titled, "*Triumph of the Will.*" Religions rest on myths of will as opposed to actualities. Free will is just another way of saying that the disadvantaged have "nothing left to lose."

Archaeologist Steven Mithen: "Brain, body and material culture are all constituent elements of the human mind."

Philosopher Patricia Churchland: "The mind that we are assured can dominate over matter is in fact certain brain patterns interacting with and interpreted by other patterns. Moreover, one's self, as apprehended introspectively and represented incessantly, is a brain-dependent construct."

All thought is embodied.

Carl Zimmer, in *Soul Made Flesh*: "Finding the mechanisms of consciousness will not mean that we lack a true self. It's just that this self looks less and less like what most of us picture in our heads—an autonomous, unchanging being that has a will of its own, that is the sole, conscious source of our actions, and that distinguishes humans from animals. All animals probably create some kind of representation of their bodies in their brains, and humans simply create a particularly complicated model. We infuse it with memories, embellish it with autobiographies, and project it into the future as we ponder our hopes and goals."

The Greek physician Hippocrates, who died in 377 B.C., was one of the earliest to question free will and to see thoughts, feelings, and expressions as embodied aspects of brain activity.

Daniel C. Dennett, director of the Center for Cognitive Studies at Tufts University: "Our widespread tradition has it that we human beings are responsible agents, captains of our fate, *because* what we really are are *souls*, immaterial and immortal clumps of Godstuff that inhabit and control our material bodies rather like spectral puppeteers. It is our souls that are the source of all meaning, and the locus of all our sufferings, our joy, our glory and shame. But this idea of immaterial souls, capable of defying the laws of physics, has outlived its credibility thanks to the advance of the natural sciences. Many people think the implications of this are dreadful: We don't really have 'free will' and nothing really matters….they are wrong.

"[Quoted Tom Wolfe from a piece called "Sorry, But Your Soul Just Died"] "Since consciousness and thought are the entirely physical products of your brain and nervous system, what makes you think you have free will? Where is it going to come from?"…

"It is the very reliability of deterministic worlds that makes it possible for organisms to extract information from the world so that they can look ahead and avoid disasters that they see coming. In a truly random world everything really would be inevitable. It is just the opposite of what people often think: a world of randomness would be a world where everything was inevitable and nothing was evitable. …

"Determinism is the friend, not the foe, of those who dislike inevitability….

"The French poet Paul Valery once spoke of 'producing future.' I like to think that's what brains are for: they are for producing future. You extract information from the past and use it to produce future, and the more future you can produce the more freedom you have….

"Yes, we're animals. Yes, we're mammals and yes, we're primates. But we also have features that distinguish us radically from all other primates. The main one of those is language, and the reason that that is such a radical discontinuity is because it means we're not solitary knowers….that's where our strengths, our intellectual distinction comes from."

Our ethical understandings must be grounded on accurate observations of the natural, i.e. the real, world and our ethical positions must therefore adapt and change as human knowledge accrues.

George Lakoff, in *Moral Politics: How Liberals and Conservatives Think*, calls for the Nurturant Parent Model, an aspect of which is Morality as Empathy: "Taking morality as empathy requires basing

your actions on their values, not yours. This requires a stronger Golden Rule: Do unto others as *they* would have you do unto them."

The merchants of immortality, the purveyors of the supernatural and the deniers of the physical world, have been telling their tales as long as man has had the power of speech. Buddhists claim a "subjective" existence separate from the physical corpus, monotheists seek it in "heaven."

Anton Chekhov: "Man will become better when you show him what he is like."

Carl Zimmer tells us that in different cultures people's brains "simply don't work the same: Genes, culture, and personal experience have wired their moral circuitry in different patterns." Princeton researcher Joshua Greene states that from his neuroimaging studies, "Once you understand someone's behavior on a sufficiently mechanical level, it's very hard to look at them as evil. You can look at them as dangerous; you can pity them. But evil doesn't exist at a neuronal level."

Terry Eagleton, reviewing Roy Porter's *Flesh in the Age of Reason*: "In its dependency, the body recalls the unpalatable truth that we are not self-determining, self-sufficient beings but creatures who draw our life and meaning from one another….As Porter puts it… 'We cannot command our hair not to fall out, tell our kidneys to secrete or our heart to beat.'"

George Lakoff (**www.rockridgeinstitute.org**): "A frame is a conceptual structure used in thinking."

FROM BELOW

10¢   all them kill

USA

Or Give Us Death

Peace by

Superior Firen

let god figure it out

DEATH FROM ABOVE

UNDERGROUND

ONE NATION

ONE NATION

UNDERGROUND

UNDERGROUND

ONE NATION

ONE NATION

Republicans and the religious right have had a long time to develop consistent and enduring frames. "The power of these frames cannot be overcome immediately. Frame development takes time and work. Democrats have to start reframing now and keep at it. Democratic reframing must express fundamental Democratic values: empathy, responsibility, fairness, community, cooperation, doing our fair share." It is complex. "Reframing requires a rewiring of the brain. That may take an investment of time, effort, and money. The conservatives have realized that." We must also commit the resources. "Moral: The truth alone will not set you free. It has to be framed correctly." "Framing is an art, though cognitive linguistics can help a lot. It needs to be done systematically."

Richard Feynman put it best, when he stated that science is the art of not fooling yourself. The siren of simplicity is always luring us to destruction on her shores.

Terrorism killed less than 5,000 Americans in the last ten years, failure to wear seatbelts killed over 160,000, failure to fully vaccinate Americans for the flu killed 300,000, problems with legal prescriptions killed around a million and other medical errors around 500,000, household falls 60,000, food poisoning killed 50,000, and poor nutrition killed many more children than terrorism killed all Americans.

In 2000, the World Health Organization reported 1.6 million violent deaths, of which 60 percent were suicides. Six million children die directly from starvation and another 4 million from other preventable causes. More than a million people died in automobile accidents. Preventable disease kills millions of adults throughout the world. One quarter of all children throughout the world are malnourished. Thirty million infants every year are born with intra-uterine growth retardation. Starvation is at a 600-year peak and deaths from conflict are at an all-time low.

Heart disease kills almost nine times as many American women as breast disease and lung cancer kills one and one-half times as many. However, we spend 10 times as much on breast cancer as lung cancer and largely ignore heart disease when providing medical care and research for women. Why? Because lung cancer is a disease of moral affliction and breast cancer is more emotionally threatening. Though it is interesting to note that many Americans believe that breast cancer results from immorality—note the attempts to "prove" that breast cancer is related to promiscuity, abortion, drug use, and other sins.

In the United States, three times as many people die from ingesting too much sodium, usually as salt, than from the use of illicit drugs. What does evil focus on? Evil focuses on what should be instead of what is. Human evils as opposed to natural ones. If we spent a fraction of the money we spend fighting 'sins' dealing with the actual causes of morbidity and mortality, the world would be a healthier place for all. Evil framing kills.

Politicians, theologians, and the media all thrive by pandering to our base fears. We evolved in an environment where survival depended on swift fight or flight responses. Our brains are limited in their abilities to quickly analyze and understand complex situations, so in their parsimony they developed a basic fear response. Feeding our fears makes for successful politics, religions, and media. However, as social beings we are able to collectively analyze and understand the real threats facing mankind and the world on which we live, but this requires questioning and overthrowing the basic folk mythologies that served our hunter-gatherer ancestors.

Evil is a reactionary, emotional frame. There is no Strict Father on high who will punish us for failing to overcome our evolved selves. We must replace concepts of sin and evil with a nurturant and positive frame that recognizes harmful actions and causes, and encourages appropriate remediations.

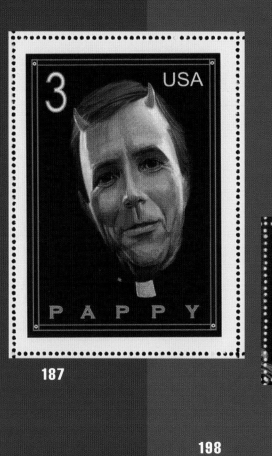

187

3 USA

PAPPY

192

194

NUCLEAR FLOWER

2004

Gogolyák post

186

THE ART VILLAGE

POST

IDIOT

1

A Fan of Ed Gein

198

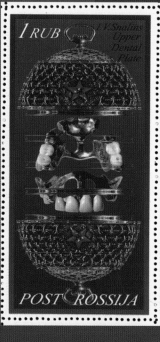

REVENUE $4

MINISTRY OF TRUTH

1 RUB / V.Snalins Upper Dental Plate

POST ROSSIJA

202

195

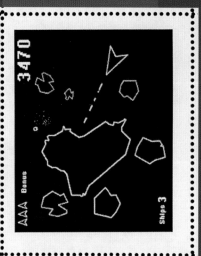

199

13 USA

redrum

190

203

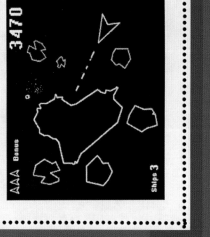

Harry S. Truman

ATOM BOMBER   Hiroshima and Nagasaki '45

Harry S. Truman

ATOM BOMBER   Hiroshima and Nagasaki '45

3470

AAA   Bonus   Ships 3

196

L   BOBARIPOST

189

204

197

JiHAD

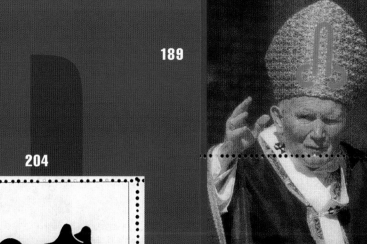

Father
John Geoghan
Pedophilie

MonotheisM
artgonepostal.com

POST
IDIOT
1
A Fan of Ted Bundy

"To define an evil in terms of a specific group, where such an evil
is not inherent in the group but capable of springing up anywhere,
is to remove responsibility from ourselves." — HOWARD ZINN

191

ND IT IS SET O | N FIRE OF HE
JOEL SMITH COMMEMORATIVE TONGUE | JOEL SMITH COMMEMORATIVE TONGUE

205

38
The WONDER of TELEVISION
PANPOST

DEADLY SINS

193

ONE NATION
UNDERGROUND

201

90 **CANADA**
PLACE
OF
RAGE

90 CANADA
ORT
DER
SKEPSIS

200

GURS - VICHY FRANCE

12.50
FRATERNITE
KARL SCHWESIG - 1941

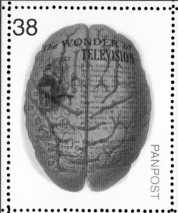

188

I BOBARTPOST | V BOBARTPOST | E BOBARTPOST

THE ART VILLAGE — IDIOT POST — 1 — A Fan of Charles Manson

POST — IDIOT — THE ART VILLAGE — 1 — A Fan of Peter Kürten

POST — IDIOT — THE ART VILLAGE — 1 — A Fan of Mark Chapman

POST — IDIOT — THE ART VILLAGE — 1 — A Fan of Myra Hindley

POST — IDIOT — THE ART VILLAGE — 1 — A Fan of Albert DeSalvo

POST — IDIOT — THE ART VILLAGE — 1 — A Fan of Graham Young

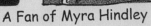

POST — IDIOT — THE ART VILLAGE — 1 — A Fan of Ed Gein

POST — IDIOT — THE ART VILLAGE — 1 — A Fan of Ted Bundy

POST — IDIOT — THE ART VILLAGE — 1 — A Fan of George W. Bush

Vittore Baroni @ E.O.N.-Italy 4 MT & MHdL - 11-11-03   with apologies to Brett Mullet, whoever he is

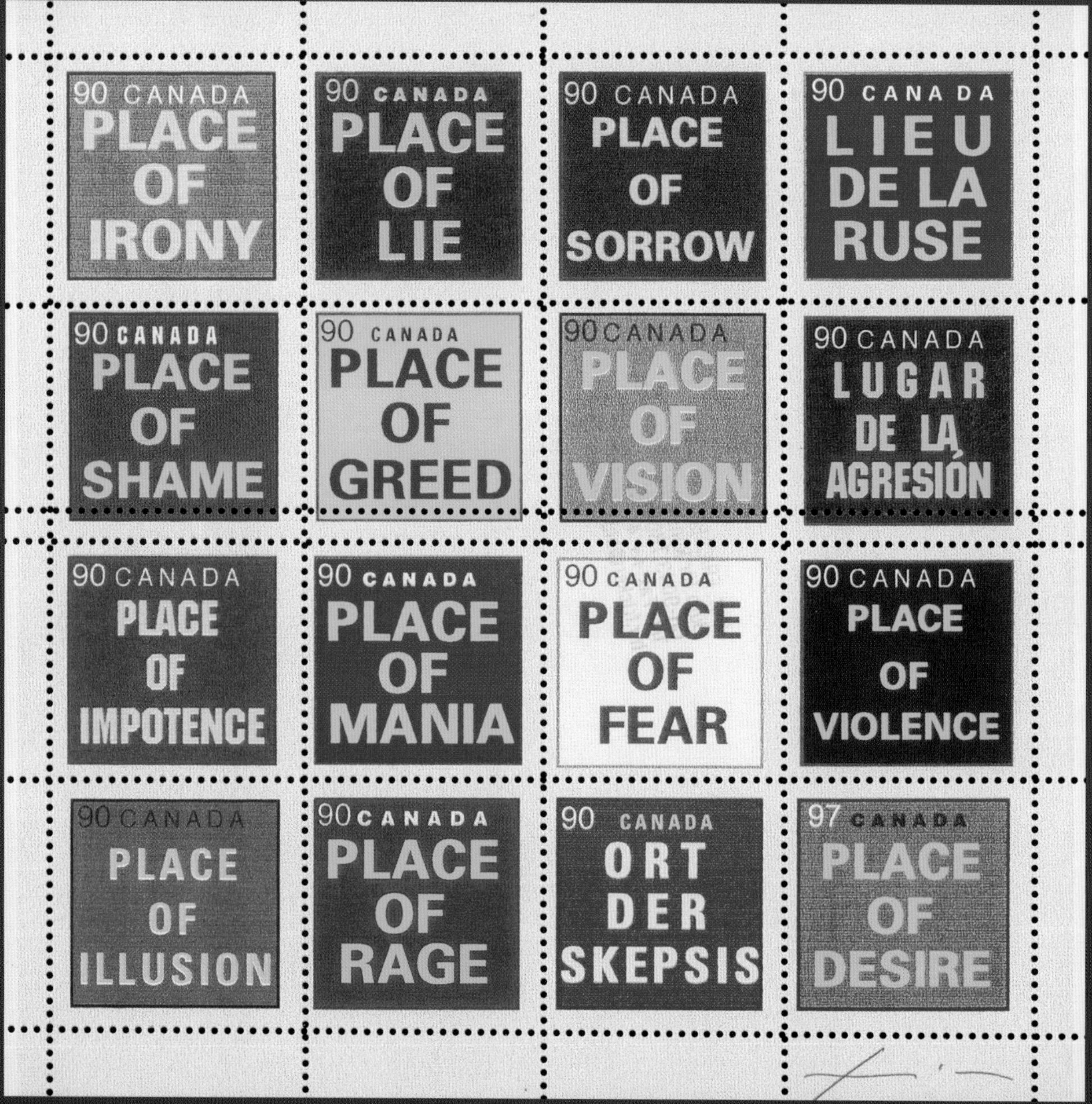

 • Place of • H.R. FRICKER • TORGEN-SWITZERLAND

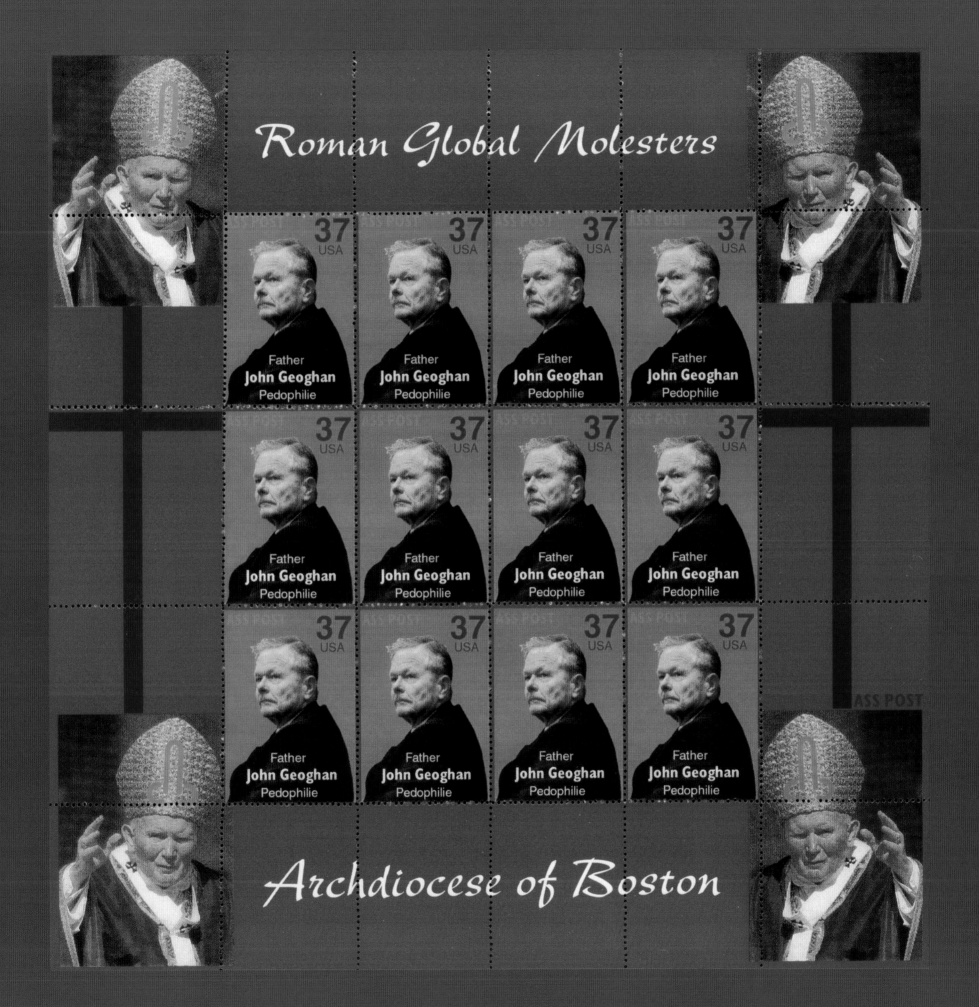

Ken McGhee

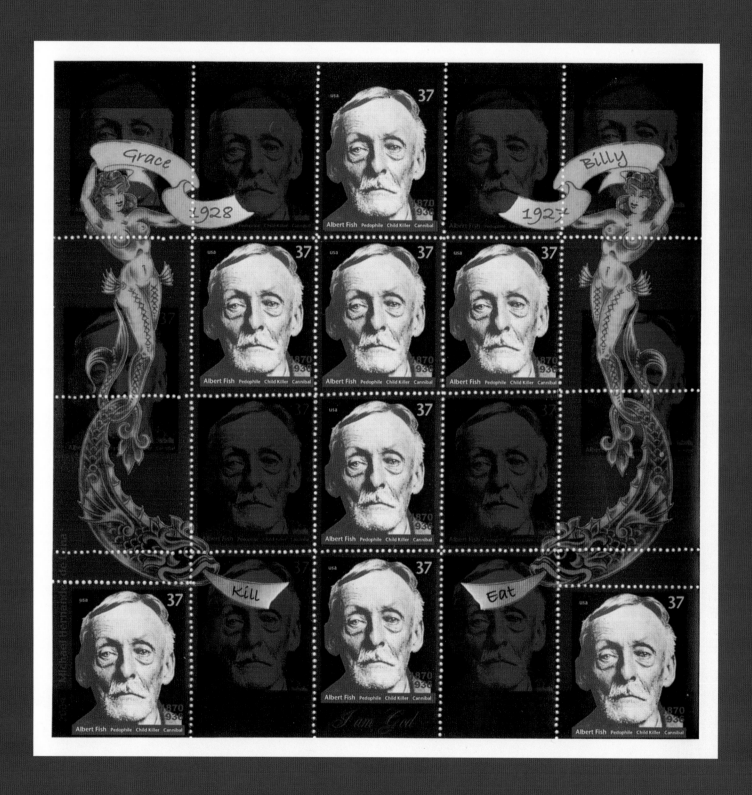

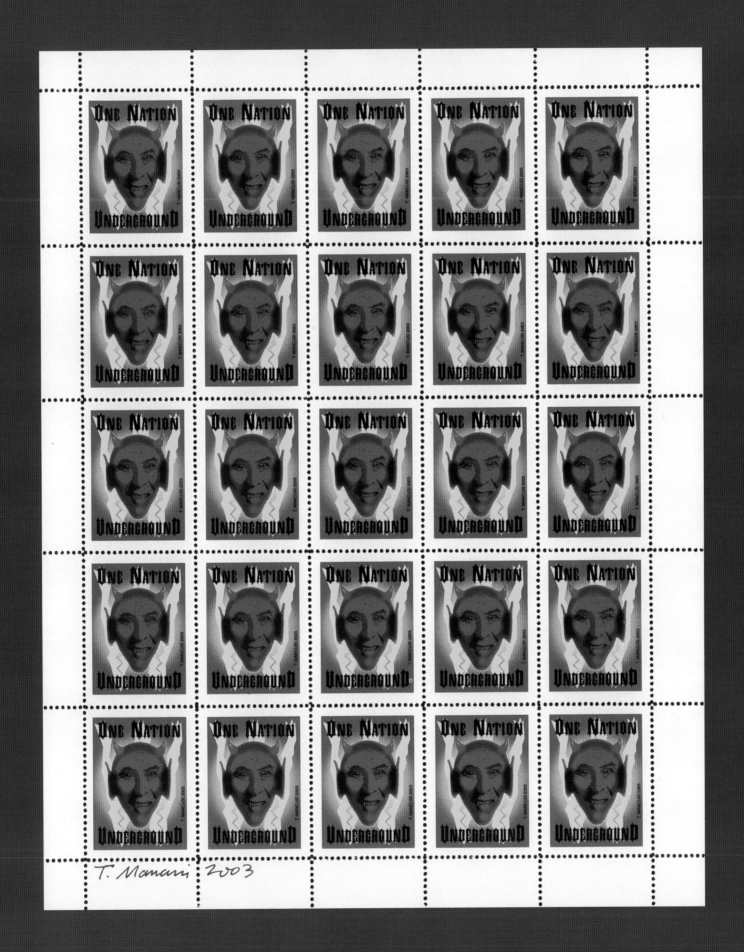

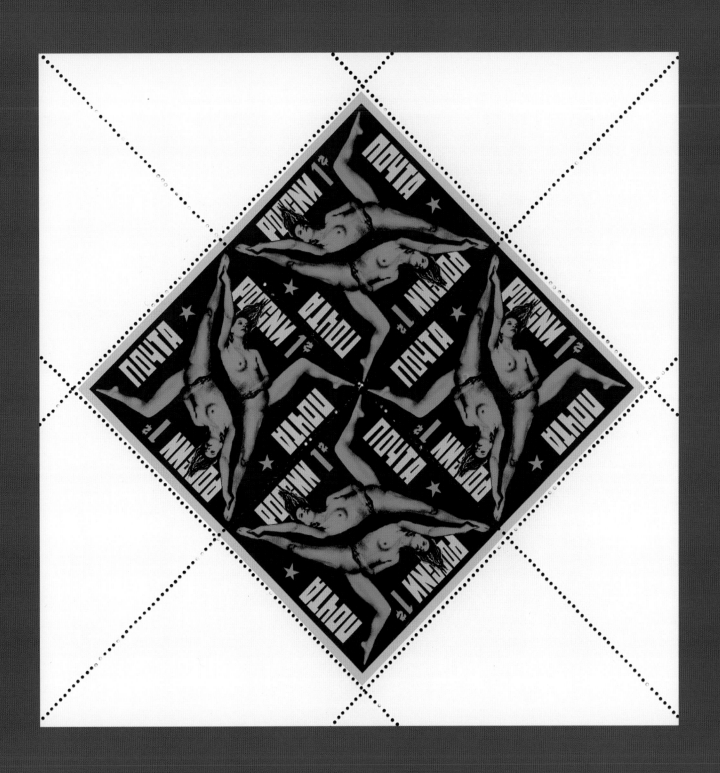

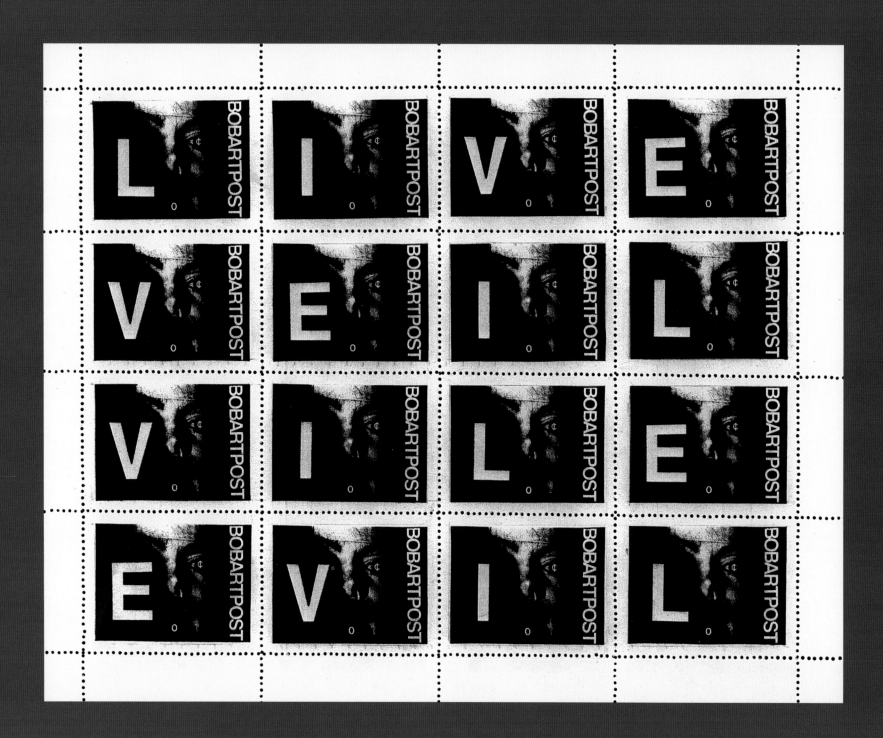

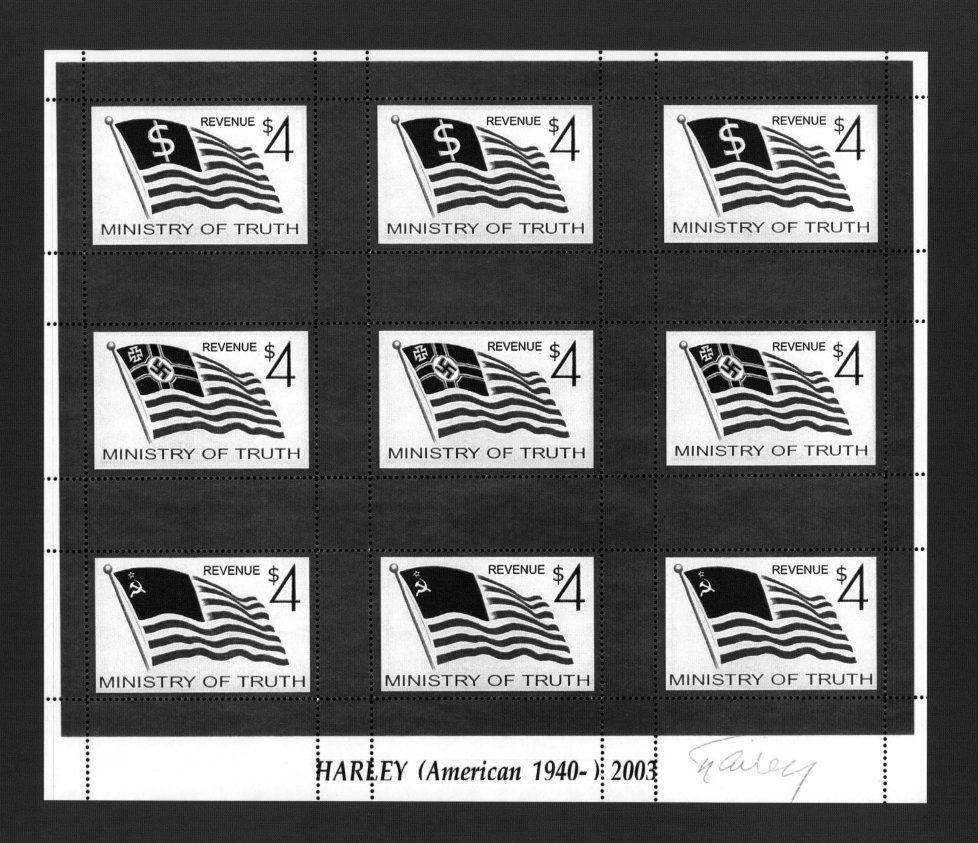

HARLEY (American 1940-) 2003

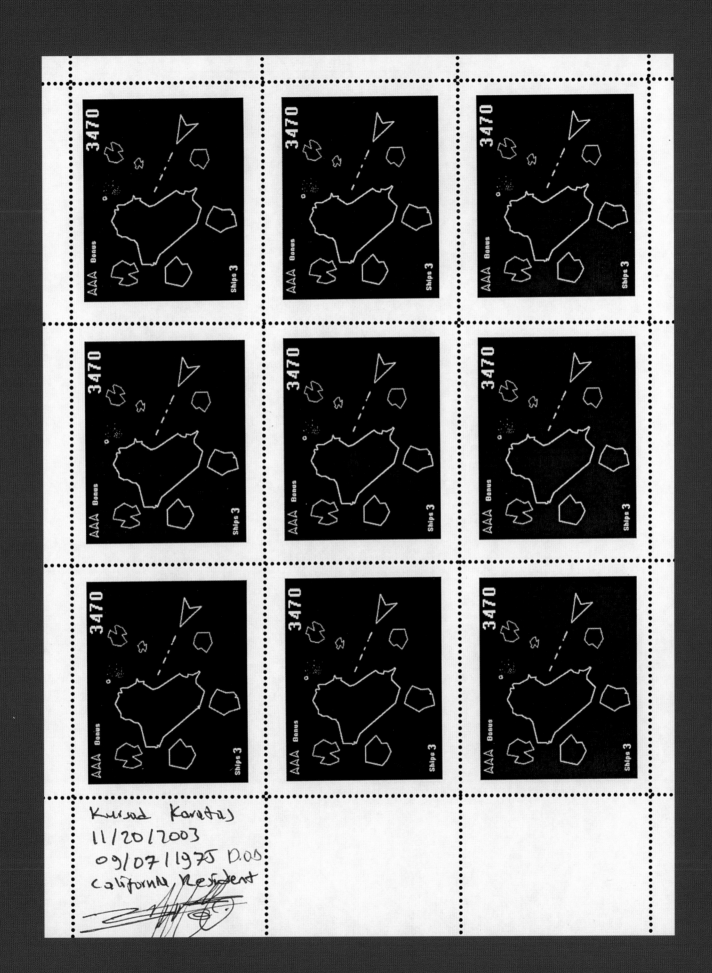

The original Artistamps by German artist Karl Schwesig (1898-1955) were drawn in colored ink on the blank perforated margins of an actual postage stamp sheet in Gurs, a large internment camp in unoccupied Vichy France and dated 'March, 1941.'

Reproduction rights to the Schwesig stamps courtesy of Galerie Remmert und Barth, Düsseldorf/West Germany; reproduction of the originals from the Collection of The Leo Beack Institute/New York. Published on the occasion of the INTERNATIONAL INVITATIONAL ARTISTAMP EXHIBITION, Dec. 7 - 31, 1989 by the Davidson Galleries, Seattle, Washington, USA.

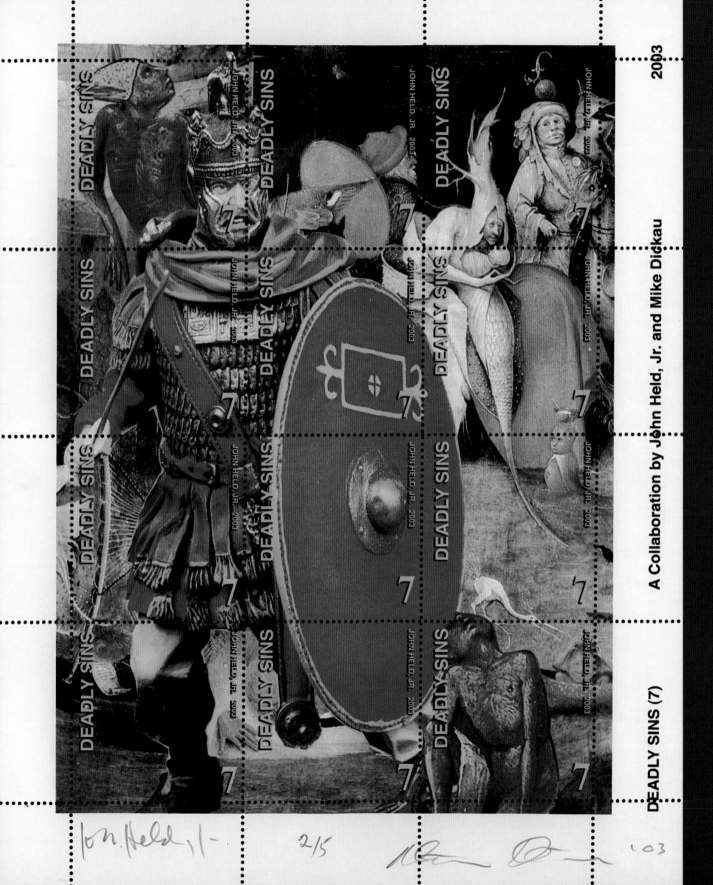

DEADLY SINS (7)   A Collaboration by John Held, Jr. and Mike Dickau   2003

John Held Jr   2/5   203

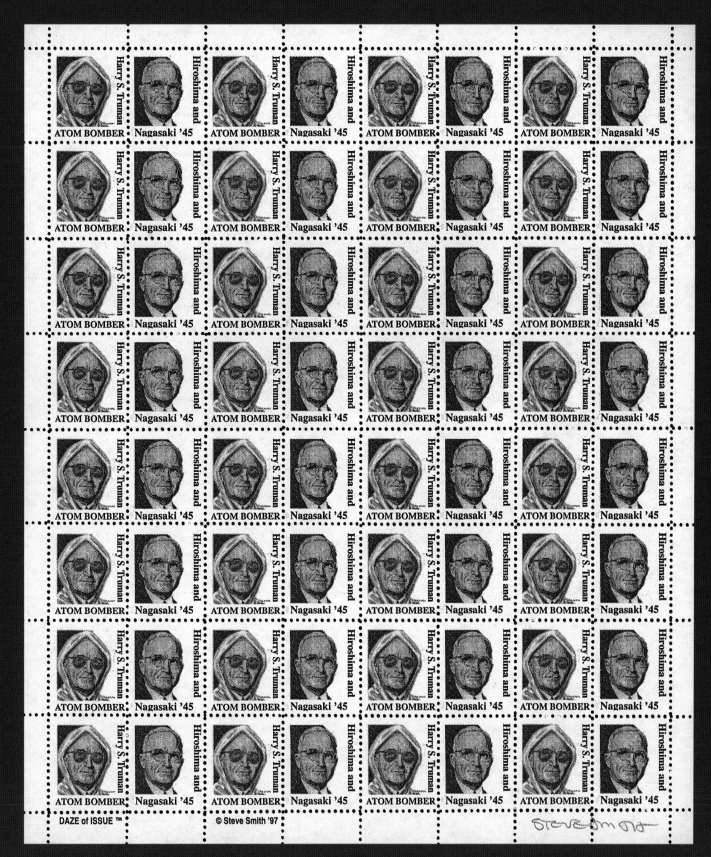

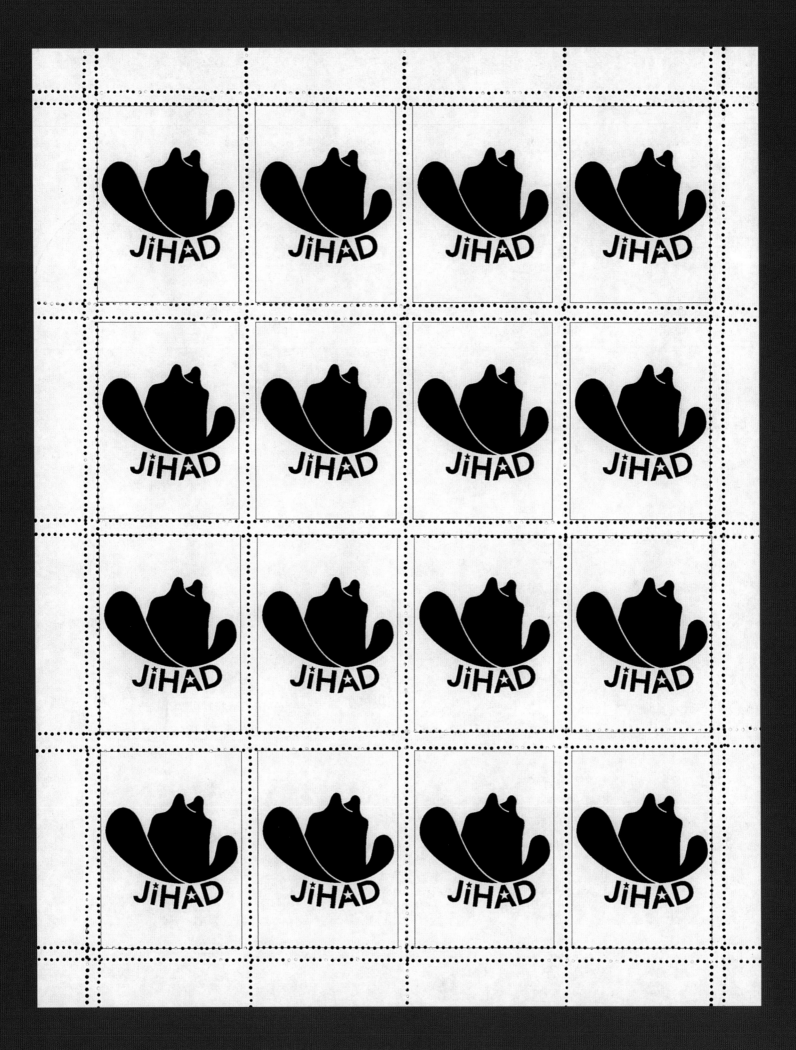

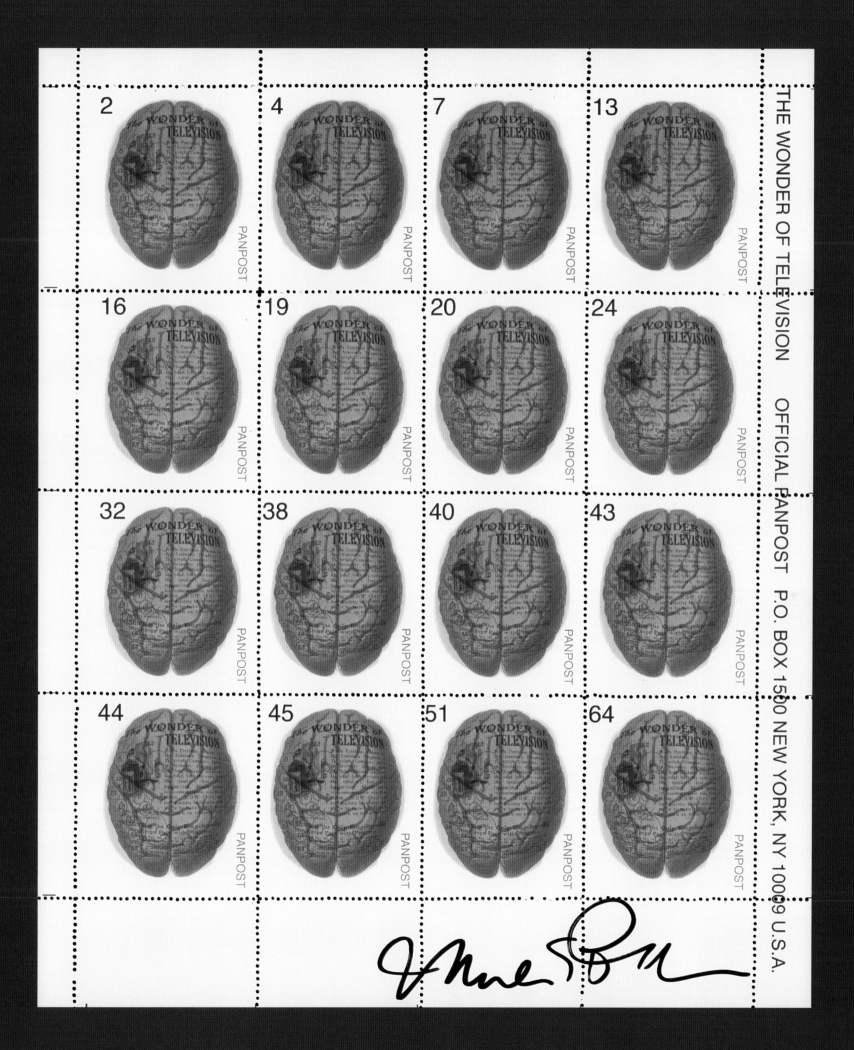

by **Claudia Alonzo**

vile

Told years ago

it happened because of a fable

a tree, a naked woman and man

a snake's wit

and the future shot to hell

Is this fast-spreading,

like a cancer?

In my family, in yours

Cells of Evil exist in my body,

in yours

Evil is something that throws people on their knees in prayer

They travel to historic lands

MECCA

MEXICO CITY

ROME

LOURDES

Faith is lost over Evil

kids lose parents over Evil

women and men lose each other

nation's leaders act with imbecility

Evil is shot into his arm with a needle

or snorted into her nose

It is given to that boy with anything but affection,

branded into his brain like a tattoo before he decides to take that little girl to the forest

Evil multiplies in the womb

and continues to manipulate

in the kitchen

and in the car

still moving

Money?

The root of Evil?

No, the handler is Evil,

the brain's mischievous lover.